Denis Sinor

Bibliography

Compiled

by

Ruth I. Meserve

EUROLINGUA
Eurasian Linguistic Association
Bloomington, Indiana 47402-0101

1986

Manufactured in the United States of America

ISSN 0195-7163

ISBN 0-931922-12-7

DENIS SINOR BIBLIOGRAPHY

ARCADIA BIBLIOGRAPHICA

VIRORUM ERUDITORUM

Editor: Gyula Décsy

Fasciculus 9

Denis Sinor

Bibliography

Compiled

by

RUTH I. MESERVE

EUROLINGUA

Eurasian Linguistic Association

Bloomington, Indiana 47402-0101

1986

Table of Contents

1. BOOKS AUTHORED

1.1 *A Modern Hungarian-English Dictionary.* Cambridge: W. Heffer and Sons, 1957, 131 pp.

R e v i e w s of this book appeared in the following publications. The reviewer's name is in parentheses.

Times Literary Supplement, 26 July 1957.

Heti hirek angliai magyarok részére (London), 16 August 1957, p. 1.

Ural-Altaische Jahrbücher, 30 (1958), p. 149. (GY. DÉCSY)

1.2 *History of Hungary.* London: George Allen and Unwin, 1959; New York: Frederick Praeger, 1959; rpt. Westport, Connecticut: Greenwood Press, 1976, 310 pp.

R e v i e w s :

Times Literary Supplement, 19 June 1959, p. 367.

Cape Times, 19 June 1959.

The Irish Press, 27 June 1959. (OWEN DUDLEY EDWARDS)

Cambridge Daily News, 30 June 1959, p. 4 (N.R.G.)

Cork Examiner (Ireland), 2 July 1959.

Sunday Times (Johannesburg), 5 July 1959.

Dominion (Wellington, N.Z.), 16 July 1959.

Sunday Mail (Adelaide, Australia), 18 July 1959.

Sphere (London), 15 August 1959.

Hirünk a világban, 9 (1959), Bibliographical supplement, pp. 10-12.
    (GYÖRGY TABORSKY)

British Book News, September 1959.

The Press (Christchurch, N.Z.), 12 September 1959.

International Review of Social History (Amsterdam), 14 (1959).

The Age (London?), 24 October 1959.

History (London), October 1959. (C. A. MACARTNEY)

International Affairs, October 1959. (ANDREW RÉVAI)

Nyt Fra Historian (Denmark), 1 December 1959. (BJ. N.)

Library Journal, 85 (February 1960), p. 655. (ELIZABETH K. VALKENIER)

Express and Star (Wolverhampton, England), 9 February 1960.

Orbis, 4 (1960).

Booklist, 57 (October 1960), p. 114.

The Annals of the American Academy of Political and Social Science, 332
    (November 1960), p. 191. (E. C. HELMREICH)

American Historical Review, 66 (January 1961), p. 458. (EUGENE GONDA)

The Slavic and East European Journal, n.s. 5 (19) (Spring 1961), p. 84.
    (ROBERT F. BYRNES)

Slavic Review, 20 (October 1961), p. 530. (STEPHEN BORSODY)
Acta Historica, 8 (1961), pp. 206-209. (L. MAKKAI)
Út Látóhatár (München), 4 (1961), pp. 79-83 (BOGYAY TAMÁS)
Journal of Modern History, 33 (December 1961), p. 426.
(OTAKAR ODLOŽILIK)

1.3 *Introduction à l'étude de l'Eurasie Centrale*. Wiesbaden: Otto Harrassowitz, 1963, xxiv + 371 pp.
R e v i e w s :
Zeitschrift der Deutschen Morgenländischen Gesellschaft, 114 (1964), pp. 206-208. (HERBERT FRANKE)
Göttingische Gelehrte Anzeigen, 217 (1965), pp. 190-196. (GERHARD DOERFER)
Central Asiatic Journal, 10 (1965), pp. 71-75. (N. POPPE)
Kratylos, 10 (1965), pp. 105-107. (A. V. GABAIN)
Studia Orientalia, 30 (1966), pp. 3-7. (P. AALTO)
Orientalistische Literaturzeitung, 61 (1966), pp. 64-74. (K. H. MENGES)
Tōhōgaku, 59 (1980), pp. 130-133. (KAZUO HINOKI)

1.4 *Inner Asia. History - Civilization - Languages. A Syllabus*. Uralic and Altaic Series, No. 96. Bloomington, Indiana: Indiana University Publications – The Hague: Mouton, 1969, xvi + 261 pp.; 2nd rev. ed., (1971), xxii + 261 pp.; rpt. (Ann Arbor, Michigan: University Microfilms International, 1979), xxii + 261 pp. + addenda et corrigenda 3 pp.
R e v i e w s :
Journal of the American Oriental Society, 89 (October-December 1969), p. 830. (M. J. DRESDEN)
L'Année sociologique, 20 (1969), pp. 283-284. (FRANÇOISE AUBIN)
Ural-Altaische Jahrbücher, 42 (1970), p. 262. (A. V. GABAIN)
Acta Orientalia Academiae Scientiarum Hungaricae, 23 (1970), pp. 378-380. (I. VÁSÁRY)
Modern Asian Studies, (1970), p. ?. (OWEN LATTIMORE)
Journal of the Royal Asiatic Society, (1971), p. 72. (B. S. ADAMS)
Journal of the American Oriental Society, 92 (1972), pp. 162-163. (IGOR DE RACHEWILTZ)
Acta Linguistica Academiae Scientiarum Hungaricae, 22 (1972), pp. 452-453. (K. CZEGLÉDY)
Orientalistische Literaturzeitung, 68 (1973), column 601-603. (P. ZIEME)
Archiv orientální, 41 (1973), pp. 296-297.
Harvard Journal of Asiatic Studies, 30 (1973), p. 279. (FRANK HUDDLE, JR.)

1.5 *Inner Asia and its Contacts with Medieval Europe*. London: Variorum Reprints, 1977, 392 pp.
This book contains 16 selected, non-linguistic articles written in English and French and published between 1939 and 1975. The original pagination is maintained. For the original articles see Section 3 numbers: 4, 5, 12, 24, 28, 29, 32, 35, 36, 42, 55, 59, 64, 65, 73, 74.

Reviews:
The Canada-Mongolia Review, 3 (October 1977), pp. 141-143. (KUONRAT
   HADERLEIN)
Orientalia Christiana Periodica, 44 (1978), pp. 235-237. (V. POGGI, SJ)
Archiv orientální, 48 (1980), pp. 365-366. (J.K.)

1.6 *Tanulmányok.* Nyelvtudományi Értekezések 110 sz., Budapest:
Akadémiai Kiadó, 1982, 156 pp.
This book contains 14 linguistic articles originally written in English, French
and German and published between 1943 and 1976. The articles, for this
volume, were translated into Hungarian. Listed below are the 14 articles,
followed by the name of the translator, the pagination, and the number of the
original article placed in parentheses.

1.6.1 "Az urál-altaji nyelvek egy különösen elterjedt morfémájáról,"
translated by MARIANNE SZ. BAKRÓ-NAGY, pp. 5-14. (3.8)

1.6.2 "Néhány urál-altaji többesjelről," translated by MARIANNE SZ.
BAKRÓ-NAGY, pp. 15-40. (3.23)

1.6.3 *"Qapqan,"* translated by FERENC FABRICIUS-KOVÁCS, pp. 41-49.
(3.30)

1.6.4 "Egy urál-altaji sorszámnévképző," translated by MARIANNE SZ.
BAKRÓ-NAGY, pp. 50-58. (3.38)

1.6.5 "Egy urál-altaji helyhatározórag," translated by KLÁRA KOROMPAY,
pp. 59-66. (3.40)

1.6.6 "Néhány altaji szarvasmarhanév," translated by FERENC FABRICIUS-
KOVÁCS, pp. 67-75. (3.45)

1.6.7 *"Taγar ~ tavar ~ Товар ~ tár ~ tara,"* translated by MARIANNE SZ.
BAKRÓ-NAGY, pp. 76-80. (3.44)

1.6.8 "Észrevételek egy új altaji összehasonlító hangtanról," translated
by MARIANNE SZ. BAKRÓ-NAGY, pp. 81-92. (3.46)

1.6.9 "Megjegyzések az altaji népek lóneveiről," translated by MARIANNE
SZ. BAKRÓ-NAGY, pp. 93-100. (3.50)

1.6.10 "Két altaji etimológia," translated by MARIANNE SZ. BAKRÓ-NAGY,
pp. 101-105. (3.60)

1.6.11 "'Húgy' ~ 'csillag' ~ 'köröm'," translated by MARIANNE SZ. BAKRÓ-
NAGY, pp. 106-109. (3.66)

1.6.12 "Uráli-tunguz szóegyezések," translated by MARIANNE SZ. BAKRÓ-
NAGY, pp. 110-122. (3.72)

1.6.13 "Az uráli és az altaji összehasonlító kutatások mai helyzete,"
translated by MARIANNE SZ. BAKRÓ-NAGY, pp. 123-138. (3.76)

1.6.14 "A *t ~ *d helyhatározorag az uráliban és az altajiban," translated
by FERENC FABRICIUS-KOVÁCS and MARIANNE SZ. BAKRÓ-NAGY, pp. 139-146.
(3.78)

2. BOOKS EDITED

2.1 *Orientalism and History.* Cambridge: W. Heffer and Sons, 1954, 107 pp.; 2nd rev. ed. Bloomington, Indiana: Indiana University Press, 1970, viii + 123 pp.
Reviews:
The Cambridge Review, 27 November 1954. (S. ADLER)
Times Literary Supplement, 25 February 1955.
Central Asiatic Journal, 1 (1955), pp. 75-76. (N. POPPE)
Oriente Moderno, 35 (1955), p. 46. (ETTORE ROSSI)
Der Islam, 32 (1959), pp. 119-123. (WOLFGANG LENTZ)
"Paideia", (1959), pp. 518-519. (GIOVANNI RINALDI)
Choice, 8 (October 1971), p. 1074.
Pacific Affairs, 44 (1971-72), p. 597. (C. P. FITZGERALD)
Journal of Asian History, 6 (1973), pp. 133-134. (G. LARRY PENROSE)

2.2 *Proceedings of the Twenty-Third International Congress of Orientalists. Cambridge 21st-28th August, 1954.* London: Royal Asiatic Society, 1955, 421 pp.

2.3 *Aspects of Altaic Civilizations. Proceedings of the 5th Meeting of the Permanent International Altaistic Conference.* Uralic and Altaic Series, Vol. 23, Bloomington, Indiana: Indiana University Publications, 1963, 263 pp.
Reviews:
Journal of the American Oriental Society, 84 (1964), pp. 82-85.
    (JAMES BOSSON)
Slavic and East European Journal, 7 (1964), p. 88. (NICHOLAS POPPE)
Central Asiatic Journal, 9 (1964), pp. 152-159. (E. TRYJARSKI)

2.4 *Proceedings of the VII Meeting of the Permanent International Altaistic Conference.* As part of the *Central Asiatic Journal,* X, iii-iv (1964), pp. 141-338. (With KARL JAHN)

2.5 *Studies in South, East and Central Asia. Memorial Volume to the Late Professor Raghu Vira.* Sata-Pitaka Series, Vol. 74, New Delhi: International Academy of Indian Culture, 1968, xxxi + 276 pp.

2.6 *American Oriental Society, Middle East Branch, Semi-Centennial Volume.* Indiana University Asian Studies Research Institute, Oriental Series No. 3, Bloomington, Indiana: Indiana University Press, 1969, viii + 275 pp.

2.7 *Proceedings of the Twenty-Seventh International Congress of Orientalists. Ann Arbor, Michigan, 13-19th August 1967.* Wiesbaden: Otto Harrassowitz, 1971, 705 pp.
Review:
Linguistics, No. 150 (1975), p. 73. (L. BAJUN)

2.8 *Studies in Finno-Ugric Linguistics in Honor of Alo Raun.* Indiana University Uralic and Altaic Series, Vol. 131, Bloomington, Indiana, 1977, 440 pp.
R e v i e w :
Ural-Altaische Jahrbücher, 52 (1980), pp. 138-140. (DALMA BRUMAUER)

2.9 *Modern Hungary. Readings from the New Hungarian Quarterly.* Bloomington, Indiana: Indiana University Press, 1977, xxi + 448 pp.
R e v i e w s :
Choice, 15 (July 1978), p. 743.
Times Literary Supplement, 28 July 1978.
Hungarian Studies Newsletter, (Spring 1978).
Foreign Affairs, (July 1978), p. 892.
Nationalities Papers, 8, ii (1978), pp. 257-258. (JOSEPH HELD)
Zeitschrift für Ostforschung, 28 (1978), p. 169. (CSABA JÁNOS KENÉZ)
Documentation sur l'Europe Centrale, 17 (1979), pp. 93-94. (J. FERENCZY)
Jahrbücher für Geschichte Osteuropas, 27 (1979).
Studia Diplomatica, 38 (1979), p. 679.

2.10 *Handbook of Uralic Studies, Volume 1, Part 1. Present-day languages. The history of individual languages. Foreign influences on the Uralic languages,* as a volume of *Handbuch der Orientalistik,* Achte Abteilung. Leiden: E. J. Brill, (in press).

2.11 *Cambridge History of Inner Asia.* Cambridge: Cambridge University Press, (in press).

3. ARTICLES AND CHAPTERS IN BOOKS

3.1 "Entwurf eines Erklärungsversuches der Pratītyasamutpāda". *T'oung Pao,* 33 (1937), pp. 380-394.

3.2 "Zur Datierung einiger Bildwerke aus Ost-Turkistan". *Ostasiatische Zeitschrift,* N. F. (1938), pp. 83-87.

3.3 "A középázsiai török buddhizmusról". *Kőrösi Csoma Archivum,* I. kieg. kötet (1939), pp. 353-396.

3.4 "A propos de la biographie ouigoure de Hiuan-tsang". *Journal asiatique,* 2 (1939), pp. 543-590. Reprinted in 1.5.

3.5 "La mort de Batu et les trompettes mûes par le vent chez Herberstein". *Journal asiatique,* (1941-1942), pp. 201-208. Reprinted in 1.5.

3.6. "A katolicizmus Kínában". *Katolikus Szemle,* (December, 1941), pp. 453-459.

3.7 "Kaukázus és petróleum". *Az Ország Útja,* 6 (1942), pp. 205-210.

3.8 "D'un morphème particulièrement répandu dans les langues ouralo-altaïques". *T'oung Pao,* XXXVII (1943), pp. 135-152. Translated into Hungarian. See 1.6.1.

3.9 "Etudes sur l'Eurasie Centrale". *Bulletin de littérature ecclésiastique* (Toulouse), XLIV (janv.-mars 1943), pp. 39-55; (juillet-septembre 1943), pp. 150-171.

3.10 "Franciaország küzdelme a nyomor ellen". *Katolikus Szemle,* (Jan. 1944), pp. 10-14.

3.11 "Ouralo-altaïque-Indo-européen". *T'oung Pao,* XXXVII (1944), pp. 226-244.

3.12 "Autour d'une migration de peuples au Ve siècle". *Journal asiatique,* (1946-1947), pp. 1-78. Reprinted in 1.5.

3.13 "Les Moines". In *Les explorateurs célèbres,* edited by A. LEROI-GOURHAN. Geneva: Mazenod 1947, pp. 19-22.

3.14 "Pierre Simon Pallas", in same volume as 3.13, pp. 196-197.

3.15 "Le Problème de la parenté des langues ouralo-altaïques". *Revue de géographie humaine et d'ethnographie,* I (1948), pp. 65-69.

3.16 "La transcription du mandjou". *Journal asiatique,* (1949), pp. 261-272.

3.17 "Le verbe mandjou". *Bulletin de la Société de Linguistique de Paris,* XLV, i (1949), pp. 146-156.

3.18 "Sur la légende de l'Oghuz-qaghan". *Actes du XXIe Congrès International des Orientalistes,* (Paris, 1948), pp. 175-176.

3.19 "Az urali~ mandzsu-tunguz kapcsolatokhoz". *Magyar Nyelv,* XLVI (1950), pp. 164-165.

3.20 "Le Symbolisme, instrument d'expression de l'homme". *La Maison Dieu* (Paris), 22 (1950), pp. 44-62.

3.21 "Oğuz kağan destani üzerinde bazi mülâhazalar". *Istanbul Üniversitesi Edebiyat Fakültesi Türk Dili ve Edebiyati Dergisi,* IV, i-ii (1950), pp. 1-13.

3.22 "Dix années d'orientalisme hongrois". *Journal asiatique,* (1951), pp. 211-237.

3.23 "On some Ural-Altaic plural suffixes". *Asia Major,* N. S., II (1952), pp. 203-230. Translated into Hungarian. See 1.6.2.

3.24 "Un voyageur du treizième siècle: le Dominicain Julien de Hongrie". *Bulletin of the School of Oriental and African Studies,* XIV, iii (1952), pp. 589-602. Reprinted in 1.5.

3.25 "Langues mongoles". In *Les Langues du monde.* Edited by MARCEL COHEN, 2nd ed., (Paris, 1952), pp. 369-384.

3.26 "Langues toungouzes". In same volume as 3.25, pp. 385-402.

3.27 "Introduction aux études mandjoues". *T'oung Pao,* XLII (1953), pp. 70-100.

3.28 "Historical Role of the Türk Empire". *Journal of World History/ Cahiers d'Histoire Mondiale,* I, ii (1953), pp. 427-434. Reprinted in 1.5.

3.29 "Central Eurasia". Originally appeared in 2.1, pp. 82-103 of the 1954 edition; pp. 93-119 of the 1970 edition. Reprinted in 1.5.

3.30 "Qapqan". *Journal of the Royal Asiatic Society,* (1954), pp. 174-184. Translated into Hungarian. See 1.6.3.

3.31 "Quelques passages relatifs aux Comans tirés des chroniques françaises de l'époque des Croisades". In *Silver Jubilee Volume of the Zinbun-Kagaku-Kenkyusyo,* (Kyoto University, 1954), pp. 370-375.

3.32 "Les relations entre les Mongols et l'Europe jusqu'à la mort d'Arghoun et de Béla IV". *Journal of World History/Cahiers d'Histoire Mondiale,* III, i (1956), pp. 39-62. Reprinted in 1.5.

3.33 "The Barbarians". *Diogenes,* 18 (1957), pp. 47-60. There is also a French version: *Diogéne* (Paris), 18 (avril 1957), pp. 52-68. There is also a Spanish version: June 1957, pp. 53-68.

3.34 "Góg és Magóg fia". *Irodalomtörténet,* XIV, i (1957), pp. 78-79.

3.35 "John of Plano Carpini's return from the Mongols. New Light from a Luxemburg manuscript". *Journal of the Royal Asiatic Society,* (1957), pp. 193-206. Reprinted in 1.5.

3.36 "The Outlines of Hungarian Prehistory". *Journal of World History/Cahiers d'Histoire Mondiale,* IV, iii (1958), pp. 513-540. Reprinted in 1.5.

3.37 "The UNESCO Major Project on mutual appreciation of Eastern and Western values". *Arts and Letters, Journal of the Royal India, Pakistan and Ceylon Society,* XXXIII, i (1959), pp. 1-5.

3.38 "A Ural-Altaic ordinal suffix". *Ural-Altaische Jahrbücher,* XXXI (1959), pp. 417-425. Translated into Hungarian. See 1.6.4.

3.39 "Sur les noms altaïques de la licorne". *Wiener Zeitschrift für die Kunde des Morgenlandes,* LVI (1960), pp. 168-176.

3.40 "Un suffixe de lieu ouralo-altaïque". *Acta Orientalia Academiae Scientiarum Hungaricae,* XII, i-iii (1961), pp. 169-178. Translated into Hungarian. See 1.6.5.

3.41 "Hajó". *Magyar Nyelv,* LVII, ii (1961), pp. 169-173.

3.42 "On water transport in Central Eurasia". *Ural-Altaische Jahrbücher,* XXXIII (1961), pp. 156-177. Reprinted in 1.5.

3.43 "Az enciklopédia írás nehézségeiről". *Nagyvilág,* VII (1962), pp. 273-275.

3.44 "Taγar ~ tavar ~ TOBAP ~ tár ~ tara". *American Studies in Altaic Linguistics,* Uralic and Altaic Series, Vol. 13, Bloomington, Indiana: Indiana University Publications, 1962, pp. 229-235. Translated into Hungarian. See 1.6.7.

3.45 "Some Altaic names for bovines". *Acta Orientalia Academiae Scientiarum Hungaricae,* XV, i-iii (1962), pp. 315-324. Translated into Hungarian. See 1.6.6.

3.46 "Observations on a new comparative Altaic phonology". *Bulletin of the School of Oriental and African Studies,* XXVI (1963), pp. 133-144. Translated into Hungarian. See 1.6.8.

3.47 "The scope and importance of Altaic Studies". *Journal of the American Oriental Society,* 83 (1963), pp. 193-197.

3.48 "Yul". *Studia Orientalia* (Helsinki), XXVIII, 7 (1964), 8 pp.

3.49 "Uralic and Altaic: the neglected area". In *The Non-Western World in Higher Education. The Annals of the American Academy of Political and Social Science,* 356 (November 1964), pp. 86-92.

3.50 "Notes on the equine terminology of the Altaic peoples". *Central Asiatic Journal,* X (1965), pp. 307-315. Translated into Hungarian. See 1.6.9.

3.51 "Foreigner - Barbarian - Monster". In *East-West in Art. Patterns of Cultural and Aesthetic Relationships,* edited by THEODORE BOWIE. Bloomington, Indiana, 1966, pp. 154-159.

3.52 "Történelmi hipotézis a magyar nyelv történetében". *Nyelvtudományi Értekezések,* 58 (1967), pp. 195-200.

3.53 "Uralic and Altaic Studies". *The Review* (Alumni Association of the College of Arts and Sciences, Graduate School, Indiana University), X, i (Fall 1967), pp. 24-32.

3.54 "Some remarks on Manchu poetry". As published in 2.5, pp. 105-114.

3.55 "Some remarks on the economic aspects of hunting". In *Die Jagd bei den altaischen Völkern.* Asiatische Forschungen, Vol. 26. Wiesbaden: Otto Harrassowitz, 1968, pp. 119-128. Reprinted in 1.5.

3.56 "La Langue mandjoue". In *Handbuch der Orientalistik,* Erste Abteilung, 5 Bd. 3 Abschnitt, Leiden, 1968, pp. 257-280.

3.57 "Geschichtliche Hypothesen und Sprachwissenschaft in der ungarischen, finnisch-ugrischen und uralischen Urgeschichtsforschung". *Ural-Altaische Jahrbücher,* 41 (1969), pp.273-281. There is a shortened translation into Hungarian of this article: "Történelmi hipotézisek és a nyelvtudomány", in *A vizimadarak népe,* edited by JÁNOS GULYA. Budapest, 1975, pp. 325-338. See also 10.82.

3.58 "Letteratura mancese". *Storia delle letterature d'Oriente.* Edited by OSCAR BOTTO, (Milano, 1969), pp. 381-411.

3.59 "Mongol and Turkic words in the Latin versions of John of Plano Carpini' *Journey to the Mongols* (1245-1247)". In *Mongolian Studies,* edited by Louis Ligeti. Budapest, 1970, pp. 537-551. Reprinted in 1.5.

3.60 "Two Altaic Etymologies". In *Studies in General and Oriental Linguistics; Presented to Shirô Hattori on his Sixtieth Birthday.* Edited by ROMAN JAKOBSON and SHIGEO KAWAMOTO. Tokyo: TEC Company, Ltd., 1970, pp. 540-544. Translated into Hungarian. See 1.6.10.

3.61 "Linguistic remarks pertinent to John Bell's journey from St. Petersburg to Peking (1719-1722)". *Acta Orientalia,* XXXII (1970), pp. 231-239.

3.62 "Teaching 'Hungary'. (Hungarian Studies as an Academic Subject)". *New Hungarian Quarterly,* XII, No. 42 (1971), pp. 37-46.

3.63 "René Grousset: The Empire of the Steppes". *Journal of Asian Studies,* XXX (1971), pp. 633-638.

3.64 "The Mysterious 'Talu Sea' in Öljeitü's letter to Philip the Fair of France". In *Analecta Mongolica* dedicated to Owen Lattimore, Mongolia Society Occasional Papers No. 8, (1972), pp. 115-121. Reprinted in 1.5.

3.65 "Horse and Pasture in Inner Asian History". *Oriens Extremus,* XIX (1972), pp. 171-184. Reprinted in 1.5.

3.66 "'Urine' ~ 'star' ~ 'nail'". *Journal de la Société Finno-ougrienne*, 72 (1973), pp. 392-397. Translated into Hungarian. See 1.6.11.

3.67 "Pusztaszer". *Magyar Nyelv*, LXIX, iv (1973), pp. 482-483.

3.68 "Notes on Inner Asian Historiography". *Journal of Asian History*, VII (1973), pp. 178-206.

3.69 "Stand und Aufgaben der internationalen altaistischen Forschung". In *Sprache, Geschichte und Kultur der altaischen Völker. Protokollband der XII. Tagung der PIAC 1969 in Berlin.* Herausgegeben von GEORG HAZAI und PETER ZIEME. Berlin, 1974, pp. 35-43.

3.70 "Inner Asia - Central Eurasia". *Indo-Asia. Vierteljahreshefte für Politik, Kultur, und Wirtschaft Indiens*, 16, Heft 3 (1974), pp. 214-222.

3.71 "A magyar nyelv udvariassági formái a két világháború közti időben". In *Jelentéstan és stilisztika*. Edited by S. IMRE, I. SZATHMÁRI, L. SZÜTS. Budapest: Akadémiai Kiadó, 1974, pp. 545-552.

3.72 "Uralo-Tunguz lexical correspondences". In *Researches in Altaic Languages*. Edited by LOUIS LIGETI. Budapest, 1975, pp. 245-265. Translated into Hungarian. See 1.6.12.

3.73 "On Mongol Strategy". In *Proceedings of the Fourth East Asian Altaistic Conference, December 26-31, 1971*. Edited by CH'EN CHIEH-HSIEN. Tainan, Taiwan, 1975, pp. 238-249. Reprinted in 1.5.

3.74 "The Mongols and Western Europe". In *A History of the Crusades*. General editor KENNETH M. SETTON. University of Wisconsin Press, 1975, Vol. III, pp. 513-544. Reprinted in 1.5.

3.75 "Notes on Inner Asian Historiography II". *Journal of Asian History*, IX (1975), pp. 155-172.

3.76 "The Present State of Uralic and Altaic Comparative Studies". In *Proceedings of the International Symposium Commemorating the 30th Anniversary of Korean Liberation*, (Seoul, Korea, 1975), pp. 117-147. Translated into Hungarian. See 1.6.13.

3.77 "What is Inner Asia?". In *Altaica Collecta. Berichte und Vorträge des XVII. Permanent International Altaistic Conference 3.-8. Juli 1974 in Bonn/Bad Honnef.* Edited by WALTHER HEISSIG. Wiesbaden: Otto Harrassowitz, 1976, pp. 245-266. For a different version see 9.10.

3.78 "The *-t ~ *-d local suffix in Uralic and Altaic". In *Hungaro-Turcica. Studies in Honor of Julius Németh*. Edited by GY. KÁLDY-NAGY. Budapest: Loránd Eötvös University, 1976, pp. 119-127. Translated into Hungarian. See 1.6.14.

3.79 "Inner Asian Studies in the United States". *ACLS Newsletter*, 28, 1 (1977), pp. 1-17.

3.80 "Altaica and Uralica". As published in 2.8, pp. 319-332.

3.81 "An Altaic Word for 'Snowstorm'". *Studia Orientalia*, 47 (1977), pp. 219-231.

3.82 "Le Mongol vu par l'Occident". In *1274, Année charnière. Mutations et continuités. Colloques internationaux du Centre National de la Recherche Scientifique*, No. 558, (Paris, 1977), pp. 55-72.

3.83 "Néhány gondolat a magyar prioritásokról az Amerikai Egyesült Államokban". In *Nyelvünk és Kulturánk*, 29 (1977), Anyanyelvi Konferencia tanácskozásainak összefoglalása, pp. 25-31. This also appeared in *Itt-Ott* (Ada, Ohio), X, 5 (1977), pp. 27-32.

3.84 "The Greed of the Northern Barbarian". In *Aspects of Altaic Civilization II. Proceedings of the XVIII PIAC, Bloomington, June 29-July 5. 1975.* Edited by LARRY V. CLARK and PAUL ALEXANDER DRAGHI, Indiana University Uralic and Altaic Series, Vol. 134. Bloomington, Indiana: Indiana University Publications, 1978, pp. 171-182.

3.85 "The Nature of Possessive Suffixes in Uralic and Altaic". In *Linguistic and Literary Studies in Honor of Archibald A. Hill.* Edited by M. A. JAZAYERI et al., Vol. III. The Hague: Mouton, 1978, pp. 257-266.

3.86 "Néhány szó a mai magyar állam és az egyházak kapcsolatáról". *Itt-Ott* (Ada, Ohio), XII, 4 (1979), pp. 21-27.

3.87 "Samoyed and Ugric Elements in Old Turkic". In Eucharisterion. Essays Presented to Omeljan Pritsak on His Sixtieth Birthday. *Harvard Ukrainian Studies,* III-IV (1979-1980), pp. 768-773.

3.88 "The origin of Turkic *balïq* 'town'". *Central Asiatic Journal,* XXV (1981), pp. 95-102.

3.89 "The Inner Asian Warriors". *Journal of the American Oriental Society,* 101 (1981), pp. 133-144.

3.90 "'Pray to God on my behalf that he give me such intelligence that I can learn fast and well your languages.' Medieval Interpreters and Inner Asia". *Journal of Popular Culture,* 16 (1982), pp. 176-184.

3.91 "The Legendary Origin of the Türks". In *Folklorica: Festschrift for Felix J. Oinas,* edited by EGLE VICTORIA ZYGAS and PETER VOORHEIS. Indiana University Uralic and Altaic Series, vol. 141. Bloomington, Indiana, 1982, pp. 223-257.

3.92 "Magyar tanszék az amerikai középnyugat szivében". *U.S.A. Magazine,* 37 (1982), pp. 81-88. Reprinted in *Ifjúsági Szemle,* V, i (1985), pp. 103-105.

3.93 "Réfléxions sur la présence turco-mongole dans le monde méditerranéen et pontique à l'époque préottomane". *Acta Orientalia Academiae Scientiarum Hungaricae,* XXXVI (1982), pp. 485-501.

3.94 "Interpreters in Medieval Inner Asia". *Asian and African Studies. Journal of the Israel Oriental Society,* XVI (1982), pp. 293-320.

3.95 "A hungarológia helyzete az Egyesült Államokban". In *Hungarológiai oktatás régen és ma.* Budapest, 1983, pp. 149-157.

3.96 "Central Asian Studies in the University". In *Conference on the Study of Central Asia.* Edited by DAVID NALLE. Washington, D.C.: Kennan Institute for Advanced Russian Studies, 1983, pp. 83-89.

3.97 "Notes on Inner Asian Historiography III". *Journal of Asian History,* 17 (1983), pp. 159-179.

3.98 "The Earliest Period of Hungarian-Turkic Relations". In *Hungarian History - World History*. Edited by GYÖRGY RÁNKI, Indiana University Studies on Hungary, 1, Budapest, 1984, pp. 1-12.

3.99 "Some components of the civilization of the Türks (6th to 8th century A.D.)". In *Altaistic Studies. Papers presented at the 25th Meeting of the Permanent International Altaistic Conference at Uppsala June 7-11, 1982*. Edited by GUNNAR JARRING and STAFFAN ROSÉN, Kungl. Vitterhets Historie och Antikvitets Akademien, Konferenser 12, (Stockholm, 1985), pp. 145-159.

3.100 "'Umay', a Mongol spirit honored by the Türks". *Proceedings of International Conference on China Border Area Studies*. National Chengchi University, April 22-29, 1984. Taipei, 1985, pp. 1771-1781.

3.101 "The problem of the Ural-Altaic relationship". In 2.10 (in press).

3.102 "The establishment and dissolution of the Türk Empire". In 2.11 (in press).

3.103 "The Hun Period". In 2.11 (in press).

3.104 "The historical concept of Inner Asia". In 2.11 (in press).

3.105 "The Mongols in the West". In 2.11 (in press).

4. ARTICLES IN ENCYCLOPAEDIAS

4.1 "Bahadur". *Encyclopaedia of Islam*, Vol. I (1958), p. 913.

4.2 "Khazars". *Encyclopaedia Britannica*, 14th edition (1959 printing), Vol. 13, pp. 362-363.

4.3 "Bitik, bitikči". *Encyclopaedia of Islam*, Vol. I (1961), pp. 1248-1249.

4.4 "Hungarian literature". *Encyclopaedia Britannica*, 14th edition (1961), Vol. XI, pp. 850-857. (In collaboration with T. KLANICZAY)

4.5 "Ady, Endre". *Encyclopaedia Britannica*, 14th edition (1962 printing), Vol. I, pp. 185-186.

4.6 "Babits, Mihály". *Encyclopaedia Britannica*, 14th edition (1962 printing), Vol. II, p. 948.

4.7 Balassi, Bálint". *Encyclopaedia Britannica*, 14th edition (1962 printing), Vol. II, p. 1067.

4.8 "Berzsenyi, Dániel". *Encyclopaedia Britannica*, 14th edition (1962 printing), Vol. III, pp. 544-545.

4.9 "Herczeg, Ferenc". *Encyclopaedia Britannica*, 14th edition (1962 printing), Vol. XI, p. 417.

4.10 "Jókai, Mór". *Encyclopaedia Britannica*, 14th edition (1962 printing), Vol. XIII, p. 67.

4.11 "Katona, József". *Encyclopaedia Britannica*, 14th edition (1962 printing), Vol. XIII, p. 252.

4.12 "Kazinczy, Ferenc". *Encyclopaedia Britannica*, 14th edition (1962 printing), Vol. XIII, pp. 261-262.

4.13 "Kemény, Zsigmond". *Encyclopaedia Britannica*, 14th edition (1962 printing), Vol. XIII, pp. 277-278.

4.14 "Kisfaludy". *Encyclopaedia Britannica,* 14th edition (1962 printing), Vol. XIII, p. 391.

4.15 "Kosztolányi, Dezső". *Encyclopaedia Britannica,* 14th edition (1962 printing), Vol. XIII, p. 481.

4.16 "Madách, Imre". *Encyclopaedia Britannica,* 14th edition (1962 printing), Vol. XIV, p. 547.

4.17 "Vörösmarty, Mihály". *Encyclopaedia Britannica,* 14th edition (1962 printing), Vol. XXIII, p. 257.

4.18 "Avars". *Encyclopaedia Britannica,* 14th edition (1963 printing), Vol. II, p. 886.

4.19 "Bulgaria on the Volga". *Encyclopaedia Britannica,* 14th edition (1963 printing), Vol. IV, pp. 396-397.

4.20 "Matthias I". *Collier's Encyclopaedia.*

4.21 "Stephen I". *Collier's Encyclopaedia.*

4.22 "Stephen V". *Collier's Encyclopaedia.*

4.23 "Stephen Báthory". *Collier's Encyclopaedia.*

4.24 "Golden Horde". *Encyclopaedia Britannica,* 14th edition (1965 printing), Vol. X, p. 541.

4.25 "Kumans". *Encyclopaedia Britannica,* 14th edition (1965 printing), Vol. XIII, p. 507.

4.26 "Kipchak". *Encyclopaedia Britannica,* 14th edition (1965 printing), Vol. XIII, pp. 381-382.

4.27 "St. Emeric of Hungary". *New Catholic Encyclopaedia* (1967), V, pp. 301-302.

4.28 "Genghis khan". *New Catholic Encyclopaedia* (1967), VI, p. 332.

4.29 "Gisela, Bl.". *New Catholic Encyclopaedia* (1967), VI, p. 498.

4.30 "Hunyadi, John". *New Catholic Encyclopaedia* (1967), VII, pp. 268-269.

4.31 "John da Pian del Carpine". *New Catholic Encyclopaedia* (1967), VII, pp. 1066-1067.

4.32 "Matthias Corvinus (Mátyás Hunyadi)". *New Catholic Encyclopaedia* (1967), IX, pp. 503-504.

4.33 "Mongols". *New Catholic Encyclopaedia* (1967), IX, pp. 1069-1071.

4.34 "Seljuks". *New Catholic Encyclopaedia* (1967), XIII, pp. 64-65.

4.35 "Stephen I, King of Hungary". *New Catholic Encyclopaedia* (1967), XIII, pp. 697-698.

4.36 "Inner Asia, History of". *Encyclopaedia Britannica,* 15th edition, Macropaedia (1974), Vol. 9, pp. 595-601.

4.37 "Literature, Hungarian, Western". *Encyclopaedia Britannica,* 15th edition, Macropaedia, Vol. 10, pp. 1130, 1145, 1162-1163, 1179, 1214-1215, 1258-1259. (In part, in collaboration with TIBOR KLANICZAY)

4.38 "Umai". *Encyclopedia of Religion,* in press.

4.39 "Hun Religion". *Encyclopedia of Religion,* in press.

5. REVIEWS

Included here are reviews of books, journals, and articles listed by short title followed by the complete bibliographical reference for the review itself. Arrangement is by the date of the review.

5.1 GALLUS-HORVÁTH: Un peuple cavalier préscythique en Hongrie. *Journal asiatique*, I (1939), pp. 317-320.

5.2 ZICHY ISTVÁN: Magyar őstörténet. *Századok*, LXXIII (1939), pp. 370-371.

5.3 ZICHY ISTVÁN: Magyar őstörténet. *Mélanges asiatiques*, I (1940-1941), pp. 149-151.

5.4 UNO HARVA: Die Religiösen Vorstellungen der altaischen Völker. *Mélanges asiatiques*, I (1940-1941), pp. 151-153.

5.5 RENÉ GROUSSET: L'empire mongol (Ière phase). *Századok*, LXXV (1943), pp. 462-464.

5.6 C. LAMONT: The peoples of the Soviet Union. *Journal asiatique*, (1948), pp. 173-174.

5.7 ARTHUR C. WHITNEY: Colloquial Hungarian. *Bulletin de la Société de Linguistique de Paris*, XLIV, ii (1948), pp. 221-222.

5.8 P. W. SCHMIDT: Der Ursprung der Gottesidee... vol. IX, Die asiatischen Hirtenvölker. *The International Review of Missions*, XI (April 1951), pp. 229-232.

5.9 MARTTI RÄSÄNEN: Materialien zur Lautgeschichte der türkischen Sprachen. *Archivum Linguisticum* (Glasgow), III (1951), pp. 98-99.

5.10 Finnisch-ugrische Forschungen XXX. *Luzac's Oriental List*, LXII, iv (October-December 1951), p. 78.

5.11 N. POPPE: Khalkha-mongolische Grammatik. *Journal asiatique*, (1952), pp. 422-424.

5.12 Ural-Altaische Jahrbücher XXIV, 1-2. *Journal asiatique*, (1952), pp. 424-428.

5.13 AULIS J. JOKI: Die Lehnwörter des Sajansamojedischen. *Journal asiatique*, (1953), p. 306.

5.14 O. FRANKE: Geschichte des Chinesischen Reiches, vols. IV-V. *Journal asiatique*, (1953), p. 411.

5.15 KARL H. MENGES: The Oriental Elements in the Vocabulary of the oldest Russian Epos, the Igor Tale. *Archivum Linguisticum*, V (1953), pp. 125-126.

5.16 Altan tobči. A brief history of the Mongols. *Oriens*, VII (1954), pp. 116-117.

5.17 FRANCIS W. CLEAVES: The Sino-Mongolian Inscriptions of 1362 ...1335...1338...1346. *Oriens*, VII (1954), pp. 118-119.

5.18 J. BENZING: Einführung in das Studium der altaischen Philologie und der Turkologie. *Ural-Altaische Jahrbücher*, XXVI (1954), pp. 250-251.

5.19 EVELIN LOT-FALCK: Les rites de chasse chez les peuples sibériens. *Ural Altaische Jahrbücher*, XXVI (1954), p. 251.

5.20 ERIC HAUER: Handwörterbuch der Mandschusprache. *Oriens*, VIII (1955), p. 316.

5.21 EVA S. KRAFT: Zum Dsungarenkrieg im 18. Jahrhundert. *Oriens*, VIII (1955), pp. 316-317.

5.22 STEFAN WURM: Turkic Peoples of the USSR. *Bulletin of the School of Oriental and African Studies*, XVIII (1956), p. 185.

5.23 NICHOLAS POPPE: Grammar of Written Mongolian. *Oriens*, IX (1956), p. 116.

5.24 C. DAWSON: The Mongol Mission. *Bulletin of the School of Oriental and African Studies*, XVIII (1956), pp. 390-391.

5.25 GEORGE VERNADSKY: The Mongols and Russia. *Journal of the Royal Asiatic Society*, (1957), pp. 101-102.

5.26 CHARLES R. BAWDEN: The Mongol chronicle of Altan tobči. *Bulletin of the School of Oriental and African Studies*, XIX (1957), pp. 201-202.

5.27 FREDERICK HOLDEN BUCK: Comparative study of postpositions in Mongolian dialects and the written langauge. *Bulletin of the School of Oriental and African Studies*, XIX (1957), pp. 402-403.

5.28 Central Asiatic Journal I. *Journal of the Royal Asiatic Society*, (1957), pp. 229-230.

5.29 BJÖRN COLLINDER: Fenno-Ugric Vocabulary. *Bulletin of the School of Oriental and African Studies*, XXI, ii (1958), pp. 415-416.

5.30 BO WICKMANN: The form of the object in the Uralic language. *Bulletin of the School of Oriental and African Studies*, XXI, ii (1958), p. 416.

5.31 J. BENZING: Die tungusischen Sprachen. *Zeitschrift der Deutschen Morgenländischen Gesellschaft*, CVIII (1958), pp. 223-224.

5.32 J. BENZING: Die tungusischen Sprachen. *Bulletin of the School of Oriental and African Studies*, XXI (1958), pp. 642-643.

5.33 D. M. DUNLOP: The history of the Jewish Khazars. *Journal asiatique*, (1958), pp. 478-479.

5.34 N. POPPE: Mongolische Volksdichtung. *Journal asiatique*, (1958), pp. 479-480.

5.35 RUDOLF LOEWENTHAL: The Turkic languages and literatures of Central Asia. *Bulletin of the School of Oriental and African Studies*, XXI (1958), p. 642.

5.36 B. COLLINDER: Survey of the Uralic Languages. *Bulletin of the School of Oriental and African Studies*, XXII (1959), p. 590.

5.37 ROBERT AUSTERLITZ: Ob-Ugric metrics: the metrical structure of Ostyak and Vogul folk-poetry. *Bulletin of the School of Oriental and African Studies*, XXII (1959), pp. 616-617.

5.38 OMELJAN PRITSAK: Die bulgarische Fürstenliste und die Sprache der Protobulgaren. *Central Asiatic Journal*, IV (1959), pp. 222-224.

5.39 V. MINORSKY: A history of Sharvan and Darband in the 10th to 11th centuries. *The Cambridge Review*, No. 1953 (1959), p. 447.

5.40 T. LEHTISALO: Juraksamojedisches Wörterbuch. *Bulletin of the School of Oriental and African Studies*, XXIII (1960), pp. 150-151.

5.41 GY. MORAVCSIK: Byzantinoturcica. *Bulletin of the School of Oriental and African Studies*, XXIII (1960), p. 202.

5.42 WALTHER HEISSIG and CHARLES BAWDEN: Monγol Borǰigid oboγ-un teüke von Lomi. *Bulletin of the School of Oriental and African Studies*, XXIII (1960), p. 208.

5.43 V. DIÓSZEGI: A sámánhit emlékei a magyar népi műveltségben. *Bulletin of the School of Oriental and African Studies*, XXIII (1960), pp. 419-420.

5.44 G. K. DULLING: An introduction to the Turkmen Language. *Bulletin of the School of Oriental and African Studies*, XXIV (1961), pp. 372-374.

5.45 N. N. POPPE: Buriat Grammar. *The Slavic and East European Journal*, n.s. V, No. 3 (1961), pp. 292-293.

5.46 American Studies in Uralic Linguistics. *Central Asiatic Journal*, VI (1961), p. 319.

5.47 ERICH HAENISCH: Der Kien-lung Druck des mongolischen Geschichtswerkes Erdeni yin tobci von Sagang Secen. *Bulletin of the School of Oriental and African Studies*, XXIV (1961), p. 176.

5.48 LIU MAU-TSAI: Die chinesischen Nachrichten zur Geschichte der Ost-Türken. *Orientalistische Literaturzeitung*, 11-12 (1961), pp. 364-365.

5.49 WOLFGANG BAUER: Tsch'un-ts'iu mit den drei Kommentaren. *Oriens*, XIII-XIV (1960-1961), p. 415.

5.50 LEONARDO OLSCHKI: Marco Polo's Asia. *Pacific Affairs*, XXXIV, 3 (Fall 1961), pp. 301-302.

5.51 A. VON GABAIN: Das uigurische Königreich von Chotscho. *Bulletin of the School of Oriental and African Studies*, XXV (1962), pp. 628-629.

5.52 BJÖRN COLLINDER: Comparative grammar of Uralic languages. *Bulletin of the School of Oriental and African Studies*, XXVI (1963), p. 452.

5.53 IVAN A. LOPATIN: The cult of the dead among the natives of the Amur Basin. *Bulletin of the School of Oriental and African Studies*, XXVI (1963), pp. 452-453.

5.54 H. N. MICHAEL (ed.): Studies in Siberian ethnogenesis. *Bulletin of the School of Oriental and African Studies*, XXVII (1964), p. 469.

5.55 B. LEWIS and P. M. HOLT (eds.): Historians of the Middle East. *The English Historical Review*, LXXIX (1964), pp. 552-553.

5.56 A. VON GABAIN: Maitrisimit II. *Bulletin of the School of Oriental and African Studies*, XXVII, 3 (1964), pp. 644-645.

5.57 C. E. A. BOSWORTH: The Ghaznavids. *The English Historical Review*, LXXX (1965), pp. 573-574.

5.58 H. G. LEVIN: Ethnic origins of the peoples of northeastern Asia. *Bulletin of the School of Oriental and African Studies*, XXVIII, 2 (1964), pp. 416-417.

5.59 GYÖRFFY GYÖRGY: Az Árpádkori Magyarország történeti földrajza, I. *The Slavic and East European Journal*, IX (1965), pp. 107-108.

5.60 GUNNAR JARRING: An Eastern-Turki-English dialect dictionary. *Bulletin of the School of Oriental and African Studies*, XXVIII, 3 (1965), p. 684.

5.61 V. DIÓSZEGI (ed.): Glaubenswelt und Folklore der sibirischen Völker. *Bulletin of the School of Oriental and African Studies*, XXVIII, 3 (1965), pp. 655-656.

5.62 ALBERT TEZLA: An introductory bibliography to the study of Hungarian literature. *Modern Philology*, LXIII, 4 (1966), pp. 381-383.

5.63 ISTVÁN DIÓSZEGI: Ausztria-Magyarország és a francia-porosz háború. *American Historical Review*, LXXI, 3 (April 1966), p. 1003.

5.64 RICHARD N. FRYE: Bukhara. The Medieval Achievement. *The Middle East Journal*, 20, 3 (Summer 1966), p. 413.

5.65 Littérature hongroise et littérature européenne. Études de littérature comparée publiées par l'Académie des Sciences de Hongrie. *Yearbook of Comparative and General Literature*, XV (1966), pp. 84-85.

5.66 Mission to Turkestan. Being the Memoirs of Count K. K. Pahlen, 1908-1909, edited by RICHARD A. PIERCE. *The Journal of Modern History*, XXXVIII, 1 (1966), p. 108.

5.67 KARL JAHN: Rashid al-Din's History of India. *Journal of Asian History*, I (1967), pp. 101-102.

5.68 IMMANUEL C Y. HSÜ: The Ili crisis. A study of Sino-Russian diplomacy. *Journal of Asian History*, I (1967), pp. 100-101.

5.69 R. A. SKELTON, THOMAS A. MARTON and GEORGE D. PAINTER: The Vinland Map and the Tartar Relation. *Bulletin of the School of Oriental and African Studies*, XXX (1967), pp. 429-431.

5.70 E. R. BEVAN: The House of Seleucus. *Journal of Asian History*, I (1967), pp. 103-104.

5.71 TERENCE ARMSTRONG: Russian Settlement in the North. *Journal of Asian History*, I (1967), pp. 187-188.

5.72 DONALD F. LACH and CAROL FLAUMENHAFT: Asia on the eve of Europe's expansion. *Journal of Asian History*, I (1967), p. 188.

5.73 JOHN KING FAIRBANK, EDWIN O. REISCHAUER and ALBERT M. CRAIG: East Asia. The modern transformation. *Journal of Asian History*, I (1967), pp. 180-181.

5.74 EUGENE SCHUYLER: Turkestan. Notes of a journey in Russian Turkestan. *The Middle East Journal*, XXII, i (Winter 1968), p. 108.

5.75 ANDREAS TIETZE: The Koman Riddles and Turkic Folklore. *Journal of the American Oriental Society*, 89 (1969), pp. 309-310.

5.76 N. POPPE: Vergleichende Grammatik der altaischen Sprachen. *Kratylos*, XII, ii (1969), p. 219.

5.77 NORA K. CHADWICK and VICTOR ZHIRMUNSKY: Oral Epics of Central Asia. *Journal of Asian Studies*, XXIX, 1 (November 1969), pp. 176-177.

5.78 R. E. EMMERICK: Tibetan Texts Concerning Khotan. *Journal of Asian History*, III (1969), pp. 182-183.

5.79 "Short notices of books received". *Journal of Asian History*, III (1969), pp. 87-92, 185-188.

5.80 HENRY HART: Marco Polo. Venetian adventurer. *Journal of the American Oriental Society*, 90 (1970), pp. 405-406.

5.81 KLAUS SAGASTER: Subud Erike. Ein Rosenkranz aus Perlen. *Journal of Asian History*, V (1971), pp. 159-160.

5.82 "Short notices of books received". *Journal of Asian History*, V (1971), pp. 82-88.

5.83 EDWARD ALLWORTH: Nationalities of the Soviet Far East. *Journal of the American Oriental Society*, 93 (1973), pp. 406-407.

5.84 "Short notices of books received". *Journal of Asian History*, VI (1972), pp. 194-199.

5.85 "Short notices of books received". *Journal of Asian History*, VIII (1974), pp. 186-194.

5.86 E. WILKINSON: The History of Imperial China. A Research Guide. *Journal of Asian History*, IX (1975), pp. 90-91.

5.87 KARL JAHN: Die Chinageschichte des Rasid ad-Din. *Journal of Asian History*, IX (1975), pp. 91-92.

5.88 JOSEPH SCHACHT and C. E. BOSWORTH: The Legacy of Islam. *Journal of Asian History*, IX (1975), pp. 174-175.

5.89 I. DE RACHEWILTZ: Papal Envoys to the Great Khans. *Journal of the American Oriental Society*, 96 (1976), p. 472.

5.90 "Short notices of books received". *Journal of Asian History*, X (1976), pp. 187-192.

5.91 GIAN ANDRI BEZZOLA: Die Mongolen in Abendländischer Sicht (1220-1270): Ein Beitrag zur Frage der Völkerbegegnungen. *The American Historical Review*, 81, 5 (December 1976), pp. 1086-1087.

5.92 LOUIS LIGETI (ed.): Monumenta Linguae Mongolicae Collecta and Indices Verborum Linguae Mongolicae Monumentis Traditorum. *Journal of Asian History*, XI (1977), pp. 90-91.

5.93 J. D. PEARSON: A Bibliography of Pre-Islamic Persia. *Journal of Asian History*, XI (1977), pp. 158-159.

5.94 "Short notices of books received". *Journal of Asian History*, XI (1977), pp. 187-192.

5.95 KARL NEHRING: "Zur Methode eines historischen Ortsnamenverzeichnisses von Südosteuropa". In GEORG HELLER and KARL NEHRING: Comitatus Sirmiensis. *Austrian History Yearbook*, XII-XIII (1976-1977), pp. 490-491.

5.96 PÉTER HAJDÚ: Finno-Ugrian Languages and Peoples. *Ural-Altaische Jahrbücher*, XLIX (1977), pp. 126-127.

5.97 JEAN RICHARD: La papauté et les missions d'Orient au Moyen Age. *Speculum*, LVI (1981), pp. 645-647.

5.98 "Short notices of books received". *Journal of Asian History*, XV, 2 (1981), pp. 191-196.

5.99 LOUIS LIGETI (ed.): Proceedings of the Csoma de Kőrös Memorial Symposium, held at Mátrafüred, Hungary, 24-30 September 1976. *Ural-Altaische Jahrbücher*, LIV (1982), p. 165.

5.100 LUC KWANTEN: Imperial Nomads. A History of Central Asia 500-1500. *Journal of the American Oriental Society*, 102 (1982), pp. 240-241.

5.101 SEVYAN VAINSHTEIN: Nomads of South Siberia: The Pastoral Economies of Tuva. *Slavic Review*, 44, 1 (1985), pp. 146-147.

6. REMARKS MADE OR PAPERS READ AT CONFERENCES
(Published)*

6.1 "Sur la terminologie linguistique". *Actes du 6e Congrès International des Linguistes*, (1949), pp. 520-522.

6.2 "A hitherto overlooked John of Plano Carpini manuscript". In II, 2, pp. 363-364.

6.3 "La Féodalité et les institutions politiques de l'Orient latin". *Atti dei Convegni 12, Accademia Nazionale dei Lincei*, Roma, 1957, pp. 193-194.

6.4 "Notes on a Turkic word for 'boat'". *Trudy dvadcat pjatogo mezhdunarodnogo kongressa vostokovedov*, III, Moskva, 1963, pp. 284-286.

6.5 Speech at the closing session of the 24th International Congress of Orientalists. *Akten des Vierundzwanzigsten Internationalen Orientalisten-Kongresses*, München 28 August bis 4. September 1957, pp. 43-44.

6.6 Speech at the closing session of the 25th International Congress of Orientalists. *Trudy dvadcat pjatogo mezhdunarodnogo kongressa vostokovedov*, Moskva 8-16 Avgusta 1960, Vol. 1, pp. 67-68.

6.7 Rede auf der Schlussitzung der Tagung (2.9.1969). In *Sprache, Geschichte und Kultur der altaischen Völker. Protokollband der XII. Tagung der Permanent International Altaistic Conference 1969 in Berlin.* Herausgegeben von George Hazai und Peter Zieme. Berlin: Akademie Verlag, 1974, pp. 19-20.

6.8 Speech at the closing session of the first Anyanyelvi Konferencia. *A magyar nyelvért és kultúráért. Tájékoztató az 1970. augusztus 1-15-3 között Debrecenben és Budapesten megrendezett anyanyelvi konferencia anyagából*, pp. 181-182.

6.9 Speech at the closing session of the Second International Congress of Mongolists, 1970. *The Second International Congress of Mongolists*, (Ulaanbaatar, 1973), Vol. II, pp. 25-26.

6.10 Speech at the opening meeting of the Fourth East Asian Altaistic Conference. *Proceedings of the Fourth East Asian Altaistic Conference*, December 26-31, 1971, Taipei, pp. 8-10.

*Exclusive of items already listed under Section 3.

6.11   Remarks made concerning Gyula László's opening lecture on "Die ungarische Landnahme und ihre Vorereignisse". *Congressus Quartus Internationalis Fenno-Ugristarum Budapest 1975,* Pars II, Budapest, 1980, pp. 219-220.

6.12   Speech at the opening session of the Fourth Anyanyelvi Konferencia: "Hogyan tovább?". August 2, 1981, *Nyelvünk és Kulturánk* special issue (1981), pp. 33-35.

6.13   Intervention in a discussion held at the Fourth Anyanyelvi Konferencia, Pécs. August 2-8, 1981: "Magyaroktatás az amerikai egyetemeken". *Nyelvünk és Kulturánk* special issue (1981), pp. 283-284.

6.14   Opening remarks: *Report of International Conference on China Border Area Studies.* National Chengchi University, April 22-29, 1984, Taipei, 1985, pp. 72-75.

7. PREFACES, FOREWORDS, INTRODUCTIONS TO BOOKS AND NEWSLETTERS

7.1   Introducing PIAC. The Fifth meeting of the Permanent International Altaistic Conference, in 2.3, pp. 1-14.

7.2   Untitled remarks by the Secretary General (Denis Sinor) of the Permanent International Altaistic Conference introduce each *PIAC Newsletter,* No. 1-No. 15 (1966-1968).

7.3   Introduction, in 9.10, pp. XI-XVII.

7.4   Introduction to the reprint of W. RADLOFF, *Proben der Volksliteratur der türkischen Stämme Süd-Sibiriens,* Indiana University Uralic and Altaic Series, Vol. 79/1, Indiana University Publications, 1967, pp. v-xi.

7.5   Foreword in 2.5, p. vii.

7.6   Preface in 2.6, pp. v-vi.

7.7   Introduction in reprint of SIR HENRY RAWLINSON, *England and Russia in the East,* Source Books and Studies in Inner Asia. New York: Praeger, 1970, pp. vi-viii.

7.8   Introduction to reprint of T. W. ATKINSON, *Oriental and Western Siberia,* Source Books and Studies in Inner Asia, New York: Praeger, 1970, pp. v-vii.

7.9   Introduction in reprint of ARMINIUS VAMBERY, *Travels in Central Asia,* Source Books and Studies in Inner Asia, New York: Praeger, 1970, pp. v-vii.

7.10   Introduction in reprint of JAMES GILMOUR, *Among the Mongols.* Source Books and Studies in Inner Asia, New York: Praeger, 1970, pp. v-vii.

7.11   Introduction in reprint of N. ELIAS and E. DENISON ROSS, *A History of the Moghuls of Central Asia,* Source Books and Studies in Inner Asia, New York: Praeger, 1970, pp. v-viii.

7.12   Dedication in 2.8, pp. 7-8.

7.13 Preface in 2.9, p. IX.
7.14 Editor's Introduction in 2.9, pp. XI-XXI.
7.15 Preface in 2.10, in press.
7.16 Introduction in 2.10, in press.
7.17 Preface in 2.11, in press.

8. ITEMS PUBLISHED IN NEWSPAPERS AND MAGAZINES

8.1 Győztes ország a béke 16. évében. *Magyarország*, 24 August 1934.
8.2 Németországi mozaik. *Délmagyarország*, 24 July 1934.
8.3 Németországi mozaik. *Délmagyarország*, 2 August 1934.
8.4 Időszerű gondolatok. *Makói Friss Újság*, 25 August 1934.
8.5 Időszerű gondolatok. *Makói Friss Újság*, 31 August 1934.
8.6 A vándorló Németország. *Magyarország*, 18 September 1934.
8.7 Búcsú egy hazatérőtől. *"Újság"*, 3 March 1943.
8.8 La Hongrie a disparu. *L'Hebdomadaire Temps Présent*, 9 October 1946.
8.9 Hogyan fejleszthetők a magyar-francia kereskedelmi kapcsolatok?, *Kereskedelmi Élet*, 4 January 1948.
8.10 Le relèvement economique hongrois et les relations commerciales franco-hongroises. *L'Echo de la Finance*, 16 January 1948.
8.11 Skull and Crossbones (letter to the Editor). *The Sunday Times*, 13 June 1954, p. 2.
8.12 Cultural Exchanges with Russia (letter to the Editor). *The Times*, 19 August 1954, p. 7.
8.13 Orientalists' Congress (letter to the Editor). *The Manchester Guardian*, 30 August 1954.
8.14 The failure of President Benes (letter to the Editor). *The Spectator*, 23 May 1958, p. 659.
8.15 Letter to the Editor on Medicare. *Daily Herald Telephone* (Bloomington, Indiana), 22 February 1965, p. 9.
8.16 Magyarságtudomány az amerikai egyetemeken. *Magyar Nemzet* (Budapest), 12 August 1973.
8.17 Letter to the Editor on the Hungarian Crown. *Indianapolis Star*, 15 November 1977.
8.18 Letter to the Editor on armement. *The Washington Post*, 29 November 1981, section C, p. 6.
8.19 Letter to the Editor: On the Road to Peking - Moscow Détente. *The New York Times*, 27 October 1982.
8.20 Letter to the Editor: International Studies. *The Economist*, 26 March - 1 April 1983.

9. VARIA[1]

9.1 Nécrologie: G. J. RAMSTEDT. *T'oung Pao*, XLI (1952), pp. 230-233.

9.2 Nécrologie: MARIAN LEWICKI (1908-1955). *Journal asiatique*, (1958), pp. 467-468.

9.3 Reply to DR. ERIK MOLNÁR. *Journal of World History/Cahiers d'Histoire Mondiale*, V (1959), pp. 507-508.

9.4 Islamic Studies in Britain. New Series. *British Bulletin. Educational Supplement*. British Information Services, Pakistan, 14 March 1959.

9.5 The Civilization of Central Eurasia. Report: *Yearbook 1964 of the American Philosophical Society*, pp. 614-615.

9.6 A szívroham dícsérete (A poem). *Látóhatár*, XV (1965), p. 409.

9.7 A report on the eighth meeting of the PIAC. *The Mongolia Society Bulletin*, IV, 2 (Fall 1965), p. 41.

9.8 Report on the XXVII International Congress of Orientalists. *PIAC Newsletter*, 1 (1966), p. 4.

9.9 Report on the XXVII International Congress of Orientalists. *PIAC Newsletter*, 2 (1967), pp. 2-3.

9.10 Translation from the French of RENÉ GROUSSET, *Conqueror of the World*, in collaboration with MARIAN MCKELLAR. New York: Orion Press, 1967; Edinburgh: Oliver and Boyd, 1967; New York: Viking Compass Book, 1972.

R e v i e w : *The Times Literary Supplement*, 9 November 1967, p. 1055.

9.11 Biographical note on the works dealing with Mongol history of the 13th-15th centuries, in 9.10, p. 293-300.

9.12 Reply to "Music for DeGaulle's French Horn". Editorial. The WFBM Stations, Radio and Television, 4 December 1967.

9.13 Miért tanuljunk magyarul?, *Magyar Hírek*, XXI, 24 (30 November 1968), p. 3.

9.14 Live interview on Mongolia, Canadian Broadcasting Corporation, 21 June 1971.

9.15 Report on the Second International Congress of Mongolists, Ulan Bator, September 3-11, 1970. *PIAC Newsletter*, 6 (1971), p. 11.

9.16 Report on the Fourth East Asian Altaistic Conference. *PIAC Newsletter*, 7 (1972), p. 2.

9.17 Important old books in new garb. *PIAC Newsletter*, 7 (1972), pp. 22-24.

9.18 What is Inner Asia? Indiana University Asian Studies Research Institute. *Teaching Aids for the Study of Inner Asia*, No. 1 (1975), 33 pp.

9.19 Homage to Alo Raun, 1975, 1 p.

9.20 Obituary. Professor Julius Németh. *Journal of the Royal Asiatic Society*, (1977), pp. 235-236.

[1]Obituary notices, printed reports, teaching aids, translations, poetry, radio-TV interviews, etc.

9.21   Statement of Denis Sinor, Indiana University, Department of Uralic and Altaic Studies. In: *The Holy Crown of St. Stephen and United States-Hungarian Relations.* Hearings before the Subcommittee on Europe and the Middle East of the Committee on International Relations, House of Representatives. Ninety-fifth Congress. First Session. November 1977 (Washington, D.C., 1978), pp. 150-151.

9.22   Az Indiana University magyar katedrája. *Hungarológiai Értesítő,* II (1980), pp. 468-469.

9.23   Felix Oinas and Finno-Ugric Studies at Indiana University. In *Felix Johannes Oinas Bibliography.* Compiled by RONALD F. FELDSTEIN. Köln: E. J. Brill, 1981, pp. 47-48. Arcadia Bibliographica Virorum Eruditorum, Fasciculus 4.

9.24   László Országh: a personal memoir. *Hungarian Studies,* I (1985), pp. 356-358.

10. LECTURES

10.1   "A régi török helyhatározóragok ismeretéhez". Kőrösi Csoma Társaság (Budapest), 9 February 1939.

10.2   'L'Ouralo-altaïque", Société Asiatique (Paris, 12 April 1941.

10.3   "Protohistoire ouralo-altaïque". Ecole Nationale des Langues Orientales (Paris), 5 lectures: April-May 1942.

10.4   "L'origine des T'ou-kiue". Société Asiatique, 8 May 1942.

10.5   "Magyar nyelv". Ecole Nationale des Langues Orientales, course taught: 1939-1940 and 1940-1941.

10.6   "Introduction à l'histoire de l'Eurasie Centrale". Toulouse Institut Catholique, 6 lectures: December 1942-January 1943.

10.7   "Correspondances de vocabulaire ouralo-altaïques". Société Asiatique, 14 May 1943.

10.8   "Missionnaires hongrois chez les Mongols". Société Asiatique, 21 April 1944.

10.9   "Mur, ville, enclos". Société Linguistique (Paris), 1 December 1945.

10.10   "Les Pygmées et les oiseaux migrateurs". Institut Français d'Anthropologie (Paris), 20 March 1946.

10.11   "Le roi Boeuf". Société Asiatique, 10 May 1946.

10.12   "L'état actuel du problème ouralo-altaïque". Société de Linguistique, 15 February 1947.

10.13   "Les flèches 'nou'". Société Asiatique, 12 June 1947.

10.14   "Les Avars". Institut des Hautes Études Chinoises de l'Université de Paris, course taught: Spring 1947.

10.15   "Mandjou". Ecole Nationale des Langues Orientales, course taught: 1947-1948.

10.16   "Le verbe mandjou". Société de Linguistique, 17 April 1948.

10.17 "Le problème tchouvache". Société Asiatique, 14 May 1948.

10.18 "The Uralo-Altaic Linguistic Family". Birmingham University Linguistic Circle, 10 January 1949.

10.19 "On Monsters". Shirley Society, St. Catherine's College (Cambridge), 29 January 1950.

10.20 "On Some Aspects of the Ural-Altaic Problem". Stockholm Magyar Intézet, 25 May 1950.

10.21 "Universities and the State". Christmas Vacation course of the British Council on "The place of the University in Modern Life", 2 January 1950.

10.22 "L'état actuel des études tongouzes". XXII Congress of Orientalists (Istanbul), 21 September 1951.

10.23 "Some impressions of the Balkans". United Nations Association, Cambridge Branch, 17 October 1951.

10.24 "The System of Possessive Suffixes in the Ural-Altaic Languages". Philological Society (London), 18 January 1952.

10.25 Title not known. University of Göttingen, 1952.

10.26 Title not known. University of Hamburg, 1952.

10.27 "Hungary". United Nations Association, Datchworth Branch, 13 February 1952.

10.28 "Hungary's Position in Eastern Europe Today". Cambridge University United Nations Association, 14 February 1952.

10.29 "Polite Speech in Hungarian". Modern Language Society, 22 February 1952.

10.30 "The roles of women in different countries". Business and Professional Women's Club (Cambridge), 27 February 1953.

10.31 "Monsters". Royal Asiatic Society, 14 January 1954.

10.32 "The problem of the Uralic-Altaic Relationship". Philological Society (Oxford meeting), 6 March 1954.

10.33 "Nouvelle lumière sur le voyage de Jean de Plan Carpin et les relations mongolo-hongroises". 23rd International Congress of Orientalists (Cambridge), 25 August 1954.

10.34 "Quelques remarques sur les relations entre les Mongols et l'Europe médiévale". Istituto per l'Oriente (Roma), 20 May 1955.

10.35 "Les Mongols et l'Europe médiévale". Istituto Universitario Orientale (Naples, Italy), 3 June 1955.

10.36 "Unesco Project". Seventh Conference of the Association of British Orientalists (Oxford), 19 July 1955.

10.37 "Le cheval en l'Eurasie Centrale". Société Asiatique, 13 January 1956.

10.38 "Les monstres septentrionaux". Musée Guimet (Paris), 15 January 1956.

10.39 "The Barbarians". The British Academy, 9 May 1956.

10.40 "Impressions of Hungary". Cambridge Rotary Club, 4 September 1956.

10.41 "Oriental Studies in Hungary". 8th Conference of British Orientalists (Cambridge), 18 September 1956.

10.42 "The Situation in Hungary". Open Meeting, Great St. Mary's Church (Cambridge), 13 November 1956.

10.43 "The Background of the Hungarian Revolution". United Nations Association (Cambridge city), 4 December 1956.

10.44 Title not known. University of Graz (Austria), 1956.

10.45 "The Background of the Hungarian Revolution". Cambridge University United Nations Association, 2 lectures: 25 February and 4 March 1957.

10.46 "Pygmäer und Zugvögel". Orientalisches Institut der Universität Wien, 13 June 1957.

10.47 "12 Months of Kadar". Cambridge University United Nations Association, 13 October 1957.

10.48 "U.N.A. and World Affairs". United Nations Association (Felixstowe), 1 November 1957.

10.49 "Probleme der tungusischen Philologie". 2. Altaische Arbeitstagung (Mainz), 24 June 1959.

10.50 "Einige Probleme der ungarischen Vorgeschichte". Universität Hamburg, Philosophische Fakultät, 30 June 1959.

10.51 "Translations in general and current translation programmes in particular". 10th Conference of British Orientalists (Bangor), 7 July 1959.

10.52 "Trends in Hungarian Literature". Modern Language Society (Cambridge), 28 January 1960.

10.53 "Lateinische und griechische Quellen zur zentralasiatischen Geschichte". 3rd PIAC, Burg Liebenstein (German Federal Republic), 28 June 1960.

10.54 "An Altaic word for 'boat'". 25th International Congress of Orientalists (Moscow), August 1960.

10.55 "Impressions of the 25th International Congress of Orientalists at Moscow". Royal Asiatic Society, 13 October 1960. (with SIR GERARD CLAUSON and DAVID LANG.)

10.56 "Travelling words". Cambridge University Linguistic Society, 23 November 1961.

10.57 "The scope and importance of Altaic studies". 172nd meeting of the American Oriental Society (Cambridge, Mass.), 3 April 1962.

10.58 "The Mongol conquest of the West and some of its consequences". Harvard Yenching Institute (Cambridge, Mass.), 9 April 1962.

10.59 "Some Altaic names for bovines". Near and Middle Eastern Institute, Columbia University (New York), 13 April 1962.

10.60 "On Mongol strategy". 173rd meeting of the American Oriental Society (Washington, D.C.), 27 March 1963.

10.61 "Die Frage der ural-altaischen Sprachverwandtschaft im Lichte der neueren Forschung". Finnisch-ugrisches Seminar, University of Hamburg, 21 June 1963.

10.62 Title not known. The Toyo Bunko (Tokyo), January 1964.

10.63 "On the words for 'writing' in Central Eurasia". 26th International Congress of Orientalists (New Delhi), January 1964.

10.64 "The present state and future tasks of Mongolian studies". 174th meeting of the American Oriental Society (New York), 9 April 1964.

10.65 "Present problems of Altaic linguistics". University of Pennsylvania, Linguistic Department, Department of Oriental Studies, 9 April 1964.

10.66 "The Mongol invasion of the West and some of its consequences". University of California, Los Angeles, 30 April 1964; University of California, Berkeley: Department of Near Eastern Languages, Department of Oriental Languages, 1 May 1964.

10.67 "Altaic words for 'horse'". 7th PIAC, De Pietersberg (Holland), 1964.

10.68 "Altaic peoples in the literature of the Renaissance". 175th meeting of the American Oriental Society (Chicago), 15 April 1965.

10.69 "Asian Studies as an Academic Discipline". A "Seminar on Asian Studies", Indiana University Northwest (Gary, Indiana), 19 March 1965.

10.70 "Conventional 'Orientalism' and modern 'Asian Studies'". 49th meeting, Middle-West Branch of the American Oriental Society, Wayne State University (Detroit), 25 March 1966.

10.71 "Trade with the Barbarians". 176th meeting, American Oriental Society (Philadelphia), 19 April 1966.

10.72 "The Mongol conquest of the West and some of its consequences". University of Chicago, Committee on Far Eastern Civilizations, 25 May 1966.

10.73 "Történelmi hipotézis a magyar nyelv történelmében". A magyar nyelv történelme és rendszere. Nemzetközi Nyelvészkongresszus. 1966, aug. 24-28. Debrecen, Hungary, 27 August 1966.

10.74 "Idegen civilizációk kutatása az Egyesült Államokban". Nemzetközi Kulturkapcsolatok Intézete (Budapest), 12 September 1966.

10.75 "Altajisztikai kutatások az Egyesült Államokban". Magyar Nyelvtudományi Társaság orientalisztikai szakosztálya. Eötvös Lóránd Tudományegyetem (Budapest), 14 September 1966.

10.76 "Linguistic Confernces in Europe. A Report". Ethnolinguistic Seminar, Indiana University (Bloomington, Ind.), 31 October 1966.

10.77 "Hungary: Ten years after". Department of Government and History, Indiana University (Bloomington, Ind.), 8 December 1966.

10.78 "Asia, Unity and Diversity". Colloquium Asiaticum, Indiana University (Bloomington, Ind.), 14 February 1967.

10.79 "Changing Hungary: 1956-1966". University of Notre Dame (South Bend, Ind.), 5 April 1967.

10.80 "The Importance of the 'Vinland Map' for Oriental Studies". 178th meeting of the American Oriental Society (Berkeley, California), 19 March 1968.

10.81 "Tunguz data in John Bell's travelogue". 11th PIAC, Hørsholm (Denmark), 4 June 1968.

10.82 "Geschichtliche Hypothesen und Sprachwissenschaft in der finno-ugrischen Urheimatsforschung". Gedächtnis-Symposium Martinus Fogelius (Hamburg), 7 June 1968 (see 3.57).

10.83 "Geschichte und Sprachwissenschaft". Deutsche Akademie der Wissenschaften (East Berlin), 12 June 1968.

10.84 "Über die Entwicklung der altaischen Studien". Ostasiatische Seminar (Leipzig), 14 June 1968.

10.85 "Nomads and History". American Historical Association, 28 December 1968.

10.86 "Trade in Inner Asia". Association for Asian Studies, 29 March 1969.

10.87 "Problems of Mythical Geography". American Philosophical Society, Annual General Meeting (Philadelphia), 25 April 1969.

10.88 "Stand und Aufgaben der internationalen altaistischen Forschung". Humboldt Universität (Berlin), 29 August 1969.

10.89 "The vocabulary as a source of information on domestic animals". 180th meeting of the American Oriental Society (Baltimore, Md.), 15 April 1970.

10.90 "The integration of Mongolian history into the historiography of the world". 2nd International Congress of Mongolists (Ulan Bator, Mongolian People's Republic), September 1970.

10.91 "Impressions of a recent trip to Hungary, the USSR, and Mongolia". Russian and East European Institute, Indiana University (Bloomington, Ind.), 28 October 1970.

10.92 "A visit to Outer Mongolia". 53rd meeting of the Middle-West Branch, American Oriental Society (Chicago), 10 November 1970.

10.93 "Inner Asian studies as an academic discipline". Presidential address. 'Mid-West Branch of the American Oriental Society, November 1970.

10.94 "'7' and '100': a linguistic problem common to Uralic-Altaic and Indo-European". 28th International Congress of Orientalists (Canberra, Australia), January 1971.

10.95 "Early British Commercial Attempts in Inner Asia". 23rd meeting of the Association for Asian Studies (Washington, D.C.), 30 March 1971.

10.96 "Patterns of Trade in Inner Asia in the medieval period". 181st meeting of the American Oriental Society (Cambridge, Mass.), 5 April 1971.

10.97 "Uralo-Tunguz lexical correspondences". 14th PIAC (Szeged, Hungary), 24 August 1971.

10.98 "Miért nincs Szeged Belső-Ázsiában". University of Szeged (Hungary), 11 October 1971.

10.99 "Barbárok". Kőrösi Csoma Society (Budapest), 12 October 1971.

10.100 "Horse power". 182nd meeting of the American Oriental Society (Chapel Hill, North Carolina), 18 April 1972.

10.101 "A magyar nyelv udvariassági formái a két világháború közti időben". Magyar Nyelvészek II. Nemzetközi Kongresszusa (Szeged), 23 August 1972.

10.102 "Hungary in the 20th Century". History Society, DePaul University (Chicago), 2 April 1973.

10.103 "The historical concept of the 'Barbarian'". Duquesne University (Pittsburgh), 21 September 1973.

10.104 "A hungarologia oktatásának néhány kérdése Amerikában". Pittsburghi Magyar Társaság (Pittsburgh), 22 September 1973.

10.105 "A Biographical Dictionary of Orientalists". 56th meeting of the Middle-West Branch, American Oriental Society (Chicago), 9 November 1973.

10.106 "Introduction aux civilisations de Haute Asie". 6 lectures, Institut National des Langues et Civilisations Orientales (Paris), April 1974.

10.107 "What is Inner Asia?". 17th PIAC (Bad Honnef, German Federal Republic), 6 June 1974.

10.108 "Le Mongol vu par l'Occident". Colloque: "1274 – Année charniere – Mutations et continuités" (Lyon, France), 1 October 1974.

10.109 "On Oriental Monsters". Asian Art Society, Washington University (St. Louis), 3 April 1975.

10.110 "The present state of Uralic-Altaic comparative studies". International Symposium Commemorating the 30th Anniversary of Korean Liberation (Seoul, South Korea), 13 August 1975.

10.111 "Elmélkedések az ural-altaji kérdésről". Magyar Tudományos Akadémia Nyelvtudományi Intézete, 25 September 1975.

10.112 "L'apport turco-mongol: voies de pénétration". Colloque: "L'acculturation turque dans l'Orient et le Méditerranée: emprunts et rapports" (Paris), 20 October 1975.

10.113 "The Inner Asian Armies". Presidential Address, 186th meeting of the American Oriental Society (Philadelphia), 16 March 1976 (see also 10.115).

10.114 "Fence, Enclosure, City". 19th meeting of PIAC (Helsinki), June 1976.

10.115 "The Inner Asian armies". 30th International Congress of Orientalists (Mexico City), 6 August 1976. This is a shortened version of 10.113.

10.116 "Indiana University Ural-Altáji tanszéke: multja, jelenje és jövője". Magyar Baráti Közösség, Itt-Ott (Lake Hope, Ohio), 29 August 1976.

10.117 "Inner Asia and the Sedentary World". Saint Joseph's College (Rensslaer, Ind.), 11 October 1976.

10.118 "Inner Asia: the Heartland of the World". Ball State University (Muncie, Ind.), 20 October 1976.

10.119 "Russian-Chinese Relations and the role of Inner Asia". Purdue University: Department of History (Lafayette, Ind.), 7 November 1977.

10.120 "Western Medieval Views of the Mongols". Medieval Studies Institute, Indiana University (Bloomington, Ind.), 10 November 1977.

10.121 "Church and State in Contemporary Hungary". Midwest Slavic Conference (Bloomington, Ind.), 14 April 1978.

10.122 "The importance of Inner Asia for the comparative study of civilizations". 7th meeting of the International Society for the Comparative Study of Civilizations, University of Wisconsin (Milwaukee), 16 April 1978.

10.123 "Western view of the Mongols in the 13th century". University of Saskatchewan (Canada), 1 November 1978.

10.124 Commentator: State, Society and Ideology in 18th century Hungary (panel). Midwestern American Society for 18th Century Studies, University of Kansas (Lawrence, Kansas), 17 November 1978). (could not attend; comments read)

10.125 "The Medieval Image of the Mongols". 8th meeting of the International Society for the Comparative Study of Civilizations, California State University (Northridge, California), 24 March 1979.

10.126 "A vallások és a magyar állam viszonya a 18, 19, és 20. században". Hungarian Cultural Society - Magyar Kulturális Társasag (Columbus, Ohio), 13 May 1979.

10.127 "The Soviet Union and the Muslim World". Indiana State University (Terre Haute), 27 February 1980.

10.128 "The origins of the Turkic word *balïq*". 23rd PIAC (Vienna, Austria), 29 July 1980.

10.129 "1956 and I: Personal Reminiscences". Symposium on the Hungarian Revolution of 1956, Kent State University (Kent, Ohio), 2 May 1981.

10.130 "Medieval Interpreters". 11th Convention of the Popular Culture Association (Cincinnati, Ohio), 29 March 1981.

10.131 "Hungarians and Turks in the Pre-Ottoman Period". International Conference, Hungarian History - World History, Indiana University (Bloomington, Ind.), 7 April 1981.

10.132 "A hungarológia helyzete az Egyesült Államokban". Budapest I. Nemzetközi Hungarológiai Kongresszus, 10 August 1981.

10.133 "Interpreters in Medieval Inner Asia". 24th PIAC (Jerusalem), 18 August 1981.

10.134 "Three Chinese versions of the legend concerning the origin of the Turks". 192nd meeting of the American Oriental Society (Austin, Texas), 29 March 1982.

10.135 "Types of food production in Inner Asia". Symposium on hunting-gathering and food-production type economies of the Neolithic cultures of Central Asia, (Dushanbe, Tajik SSR, USSR), 9 April 1982.

10.136 "Some thoughts on the origin of the Türks". 25th PIAC (Uppsala), 9 June 1982.

10.137 "Egy agyzsoldos naplójából". A Magyar Nyelv és Kultúra Franciaországi Baráti Köre (Paris), 21 June 1982.

10.138 "Hungary". Mature Living Seminars: "Hope amid Turmoil", Marian College (Indianapolis), 21 September 1982.

10.139 "Afghanistan". Mature Living Seminars: "Hope amid Turmoil", Marian College (Indianapolis), 19 October 1982.

10.140 "The Mongols in Europe". University of Kansas: Center for East Asian Studies, Center for Humanistic Studies (Lawrence, Kansas), 25 October 1982.

10.141 "The International Role of the Mongolian People's Republic".
Woodrow Wilson International Center for Scholars (Washington, D.C.),
5 January 1983.

10.142 "Central Asian Studies in the University". Conference on the
Study of Central Asia, Kennan Institute for Advanced Russian Studies
(Washington, D.C.), 11 March 1983.

10.143 "The Bird that Saved the Life of Chinggis Khan". 193rd meeting
of the American Oriental Society (Baltimore), 21 March 1983.

10.144 "The Mongolian People's Republic: a Profile". Cosmos Club
Noon Forum (Washington, D.C.), 8 March 1983.

10.145 "Pre-Turkish Turkic Presence in the Region of the Mediterranean
and the Black Sea". First International Conference on Turkic Studies, Indiana
University (Bloomington, Ind.), 19 May 1983.

10.146 "A tolmácsok szerepe a középkori Belső Ázsiában". Magyar
Tudományos Akadémia, 20 June 1983.

10.147 "'Umay', a Mongol term in Old Turkic". 25th PIAC (Chicago),
August 1983.

10.148 "On the earliest habitats of the Turkic peoples". 31st International
Congress of the Human Sciences in Asia and North Africa (Tokyo-Kyoto),
2 September 1983.

10.149 "Altaic Studies in the United States". "International Kuriltay".
Haneda Memorial Hall (Kyoto), 5 September 1983.

10.150 "The Concept of Inner Asia". Hokkaido University (Sapporo,
Japan), 9 September 1983.

10.151 "Muslims in the USSR". Seminar: Religion and National Identity
in the Soviet Union and Eastern Europe. Russian and East European Institute,
Indiana University (Bloomington, Ind.), 12 November 1983.

10.152 "Joys and sorrows editing the *Journal of Asian History*". International Association of Historians of Asia (Manila, The Philippines), 23
November 1983.

10.153 "The Road Across the Top of the World: The Karakorum
Highway". Public Lecture, Office of Research and Graduate Development,
The University Club, Indiana University (Bloomington, Ind.), 17 January 1984.

10.154 "The Karakorum Highway". The Explorers Club, Washington,
D.C. Group, 14 March 1984.

10.155 "The Road Across the Top of the World: The Karakorum
Highway". Plenary Session of the 194th meeting of the American Oriental
Society (Seattle), 27 March 1984. Lecture repeated in The Honors Program
Departmental Visiting Scholar in History, Southern Oregon State College
(Ashland, Oregon), 29 March 1984.

10.156 "Hullabaloo about 'hullabaloo'". 194th meeting of the American
Oriental Society (Seattle), 27 March 1984.

10.157 "Belső Ázsia és a magyar őstörténet". Magyar őstörténet és
nemzeti tudat. Tudományos Konferencia (Budapest), 10 April 1984.

10.158 "'Umay', a Mongol spirit honored by the Türks". International Conference on China Border Area Studies (Taipei, Taiwan), 24 April 1984.

10.159 "The economic aspects of Inner Asian History". Institute of History of the Chinese Academy of Social Sciences (Peking), 5 May 1984.

10.160 "The Earliest Turks in Chinese Turkestan". Government Guesthouse (Urumchi, Sinxiang), 10 May 1984.

10.161 "Mongol studies in the West". Inner Mongolian Branch of the Chinese Academy (Huhhot, Inner Mongolia), 13 May 1984.

10.162 "Skull and Crossbones". 27th PIAC (Walberberg, Federal Republic of Germany), 14 June 1984.

10.163 "Út a világ tetejére". Magyar Tudományos Akadémia Nyelv és Irodalomtudományi Osztálya, 27 June 1984.

10.164 "The Problem of the Uralic-Altaic linguistic relationship". Institut Jazykoznanija, Akademii nauk SSSR (Moscow), 3 July 1984.

10.165 "The Karakorum Highway". Institut vostokovedenija, Akademii nauk SSSR (Moscow), 4 July 1984.

10.166 "Inner Asian Studies in the U.S.". Institut etnografija, Akademii nauk SSSR (Moscow), 11 July 1984.

10.167 "The Mongols and the West". Medieval Academy of America (Bloomington, Ind.), 11 April 1985.

10.168 "Diplomatic Usage in Medieval Inner Asia". 195th meeting of the American Oriental Society (Ann Arbor, Michigan), 15 April 1985.

10.169 "The Scope of Hungarian Studies". American Hungarian Educators Association (Bloomington, Ind.), 26 April 1985.

10.170 "Gesandtschaftsverkehr im mittelalterlichen Mittelasien". Public Lecture, University of Frankfurt (Frankfurt, Federal Republic of Germany), 4 July 1985.

10.171 "An Inner Asian Story in 13th Century Italian Literature". 28th meeting of the PIAC (Venice, Italy), 10 July 1985.

10.172 "Az ural-altaji nyelvrokonság kérdéséhez". 5th International Finno-Ugric Congress (Syktyvkar, USSR), 26 July 1985.

10.173 "Keynote Address". 5th Anyanyelvi Konferencia (Veszprém, Hungary), 5-10 August 1985.

10.174 "On the Problems of Multilingualism in Central Asia and the Use of Interpreters". (Alma Ata, USSR), 18 September 1985.

11. EDITOR (Series, Journals, etc.)

11.1 *Permanent International Altaistic Conference Newsletter,* 1966-
11.2 *Journal of Asian History,* 1967-
11.3 Reprint Series *Speculum Historiale,* (New York: Barnes and Noble):
    11.3.1 C. C. MIEROW, *The Gothic History of Jordanes,* (1915; rpt. 1960).
    11.3.2 R. L. POOLE, *Illustrations of the History of Medieval Thought and Learning,* (1920; rpt. 1960).
    11.3.3 C. BUTLER, *Benedictine Monachism,* (1924; rpt. 1961).
    11.3.4 W. MILLER, *Latins in the Levant (1204-1556),* (1908; rpt. 1964)
    11.3.5 E. K. CHAMBERS, *Arthur of Britain,* (1927; rpt. 1964).
    11.3.6 M. V. CLARKE, *The Medieval City State,* (1926; rpt. 1966).
    11.3.7 S. J. CRAWFORD, *Anglo-Saxon Influences on Western Christendom 600-800,* (1933; rpt. 1966).
    11.3.8 PAUL VINOGRADOFF, *Roman Law in Medieval Europe,* (1929; rpt. 1968).
11.4 *Asian Studies Reprint Series,* 1967-1981.
11.5 *Oriental Series,* Asian Studies Research Institute, Indiana University, 1968-1979.
11.6 *Occasional Papers,* Asian Studies Research Institute, Indiana University, 1968-1979.
11.7 *Indiana University Uralic and Altaic Series,* Research Institute for Inner Asian Studies, Indiana University, 1979-1981, 1985-

11.8 On the Editorial Boards of:
    11.8.1 *UNESCO History of the Civilizations of Inner Asia,* Vice-Chairman 1981-
    11.8.2 *Handbuch der Orientalistik,* 1984
    11.8.3 *The Comparative Civilizations Review*
    11.8.4 *Hungarian Studies,* 1985-
    Chairman of the Board of Editors
    11.8.5 *Ural-Altaische Jahrbücher, Pars Altaica,* 1964-1966

12. COURSES TAUGHT AT INDIANA UNIVERSITY
(by academic year)

1961-1962: Mongols and Medieval Europe
Altaic Languages

1962-1963: Inner Asian History and Civilization before the Mongol Conquest
Uralic and Altaic Political Structures
3rd Year Hungarian I-II
Hungarian History and Civilization
Comparative Altaic Phonology

1963-1964: Mongols and Medieval Europe
Comparative Altaic Morphology I-II
Elementary Hungarian I-II
Hungarian History and Civilization
Seminar in Hungarian Studies
3rd Year Hungarian I-II

1964-1965: Inner Asian History and Civilization before the Mongol Conquest
Hungarian History and Civilization
Individual Readings in History
Seminar in Hungarian Studies
Seminar in Altaic Studies
Uralic and Altaic Political Structures
Altaic Languages
3rd Year Hungarian I (With Laszlo Kovács) - II
2nd Year Hungarian I-II (with Epstein)
Elementary Hungarian I-II

1965-1966: Mongols and Medieval Europe
3rd Year Hungarian I-II
Elementary Hungarian I-II
Hungarian History and Civilization
Comparative Altaic Phonology
Seminar in Hungarian Studies

Sum. 1966: Research in Uralic and Altaic Linguistics

1966-1967: Colloquium Asiaticum (both semesters)
Uralic and Altaic Political Structures
Hungary in the 20th Century
Altaic Languages

Sum. 1967: Uralic and Altaic Political Structures
History of Central Asia

1967-1968: Colloquium in Uralic and Altaic History: Bibliography of Turkic
            and Mongol History
            Seminar in Hungarian Studies
            Seminar in Altaic Studies

Sum. 1968: Hungary in the 20th Century

1968-1969: Sabbatical Year

1969-1970: Inner Asian History and Civilization before the Mongol Conquest
            Comparative Altaic Phonology
            Seminar in Hungarian Studies
            Hungarian History and Civilization

1970-1971: Uralic-Altaic Political Structures
            Mongols and Medieval Europe
            Hungarian History and Civilization to 1526
            Altaic Languages (with W. Reese)

1971-1972: Aspects of Inner Asian Civilization: Art, Religion and Material
            Culture (with L. Clark)
            Hungary in the 20th Century
            Introduction to Manchu I (with J. Hangin)
            Comparative Turkic

1972-1973: Inner Asian History and Civilization before the Mongol Conquest
            Topics: Readings in Classical and Modern Uighur (with L. Clark)
            Hungarian Readings
            Hungarian History and Civilization
            Seminar in Inner Asian Studies

1973-1974: Civilization of Inner Asia
            Hungarian History and Civilization to 1526

1974-1975: Mongols and Medieval Europe
            Hungary in the 20th Century

1975-1976: Sabbatical (fall semester only)
            Hungarian History and Civilization

1976-1977: Inner Asian History and Civilization before the Mongol Conquest
            Hungarian History and Civilization to 1526
            Seminar on Inner Asian History

1977-1978: Mongols and Medieval Europe
            Hungary in the 20th Century
            Seminar in Hungarian Studies

1978-1979: Civilization of Inner Asia
            Hungarian History and Civilization

1979-1980: Inner Asian History and Civilization before the Mongol Conquest
            Hungarian History and Civilization to 1526

1980-1981: Uralic and Altaic Political Structures
            Altaic Languages
            Hungary in the 20th Century

1981-1982: Sabbatical Year

1982-1983: Uralic and Altaic Political Structures
            Seminar in Inner Asian Studies
            Altaic Languages

1983-1984: On Leave (Fall semester only)
            Civilizations of Inner Asia
            Relations of Uralic and Altaic

1984-1985: Contemporary Uralic and Altaic Peoples
            Altaic Languages

1985-1986: On Leave (Fall semester only)
            Inner Asian History and Civilization before the Mongol Conquest

13. DOCTORAL DISSERTATIONS AND MASTERS THESES CHAIRED OR DIRECTED AT INDIANA UNIVERSITY

13.1 AMES, EVAN B.: *Hungarian-Slovak Relations to Trianon: The Feasibility of Revision.* M.A. (June, 1966).

13.2 BATTERSBY, HAROLD R.: *The Uzbek Novel as a Source of Information Concerning Material Culture: Uzbek Town Planning, Urban Development and Structures Based on Information Given in Asqad Mukhtor's Novel, "Sisters."* Ph.D. (March, 1969).

13.3 BEKE, GIZELLE T.: *Emperor Joseph II: Tragic Hero of Two Hungarian Historical Dramas.* M.A. (January, 1970).

13.4 BROWN, BESS ANN: *The Emancipation of the Peasants of North Hungary in 1848: A Study in Social Reform and Nationalism.* Ph.D. (February, 1979).

13.5 BROWN, BESS ANN: *The National Communists and Uzbekistan.* M.A. (November, 1971).

13.6 CLARK, LARRY VERNON: *Introduction to the Uyghur Civil Documents of East Turkestan (13th-14th cc.).* Ph.D. (May, 1975).

13.7 DAVIS, MARK LOGAN: *An Investigation of the Pamphlet Entitled 'The Demands of the Malecontents.'* M.A. (September, 1974).

13.8 ERICKSON, CARL ROBERT: *Frigyes Karinthy: His Search for Objectivity as Reflected in Six Major Works.* M.A. (August, 1976).

13.9 EWING, THOMAS E.: *Chinese and Russian Policies in Outer Mongolia 1911 to 1921.* Ph.D. (October, 1977).

13.10 GRUPPER, SAMUEL MARTIN: *The Manchu Imperial Cult of the Early Ch'ing Dynasty: Texts and Studies on the Tantric Sanctuary of Mahākāla at Mukden.* Ph.D. (March, 1980).

13.11 HEINKELE, BARBARA M.: *They Lived in the Open Fields. The Tatars in Sixteenth Century English Travel Accounts.* M.A. (August, 1969).

13.12 JÁNOSI, ILONA: *László Moholy-Nagy: His Early Life in Hungary (1895-1919).* M.A. (May, 1979).

13.13 JORGESON, RAY JEAN-HAROLD: *The Background of the Mission of John of Plano Carpini to the Mongols.* M.A. (August, 1978).

13.14 KAZÁR, LAJOS: *The Idea of "Ability" as Expressed in Hungarian and English: A Contrastive Study.* M.A. (April, 1972).

13.15 KAZÁR, LAJOS: *Uralic-Japanese Linguistic Relations: A Preliminary Investigation.* Ph.D. (May, 1974).

13.16 KIYOSE, GISABURO N.: *A Study of the Jurchen Language and Script in the Hua-i I-yü, with Special Reference to the Problem of its Decipherment.* Ph.D. (April, 1973).

13.17 LEE, SANG-IL: *An Examination of 'Studies in Korean Etymology' by G. J.Ramstedt.* Ph.D. (January, 1978).

13.18 LIPPARD, BRUCE G.: *The Mongols and Byzantium, 1243-1341.* Ph.D. (December, 1983).

13.19 LUDANYI, JULIANNA: *A Grammatical Analysis of Selected Hungarian Historical Texts.* M.A. (October, 1977).

13.20 MARUM, ANDREW W.: *Turkish Politics in Transition: A Study of Turkish Government between August 1908 and February 1909.* M.A. (April, 1970).

13.21 MEDYESY, LASLO M.: *Evolution of the Socialist "New Man" in Hungary. A Study of Political Socialization of the Post-1956 Generation.* Ph.D. (October, 1975).

13.22 MESERVE, RUTH I.: *The Inhospitable Land of the Barbarian.* M.A. (June, 1983).

13.23 MILLER, MICHAEL GRIMM: *The Karamanli-Turkish Texts: The Historical Changes in Their Script and Phonology.* Ph.D. (August, 1974).

13.24 MOSES, LARRY WILLIAM: *Revolutionary Mongolia Chooses a Faith: Lamaism or Leninism.* Ph.D. (June, 1972).

13.25 PENROSE G. LARRY: *A Comparison of the Oguz Legends of Abu-l-Gazi and Rashid ad-Din.* M.A. (October, 1968).

13.26 PENROSE, GEORGE LARRY: *The Politics of Genealogy. An Historical Analysis of Abu'l-Gazi's 'Shejere-i Terekima'.* Ph.D. (June, 1975).

13.27 REESE, WILLIAM W.: *Some Notes on the Khoy Dialect of Persian Azerbaijani.* M.A. (December, 1970).

13.28 REYNARD, MIKKI: *The English Equivalents of Hungarian Már.* M.A. (December, 1968).

13.29 STAATS, DAVID R.: *Studies on the Mahbubu'l-qulub or Mir 'Ali Shir Navayi.* M.A. (February, 1974).

13.30 SZIMONISZ, LASZLO: *An Historical Presentation and Analysis of the Emergence of Seljuk Power.* M.A. (May, 1965).

13.31 YARWOOD, WILLIAM A.: *An Analysis of 'A tardi helyzet. The Situation in Tard.'* M.A. (September, 1966).

14. MEMBERSHIP IN LEARNED SOCIETIES WITH OFFICES HELD

International

Permanent International Altaistic Conference, 1957-
  Secretary General 1960-

Societas Uralo-Altaica, 1954-
  Vice-President 1964-

Union Internationale des Orientalistes (UNESCO/CIPSH)
  Secretary 1954-1964

International Association for Hungarian Studies
  Vice-President 1977-

U.S.A.

American Oriental Society, 1954-
  Vice-President of Mid-West Branch 1967-1968
  President of Mid-West Branch 1968-1970
  Chairman of the Regional Committee Inner Asia 1969-1985
  Vice-President of the Society 1974-1975
  President of the Society 1975-1976
  Member, Board of Directors 1968-

Association for Asian Studies, 1965-
  Chairman, Committee on International Liaison 1969-1972
  Chairman, Inner Asian Development Committee 1973-1976
  Member, Committee for Elementary and Secondary Education 1979-1980

The Tibet Society, 1967-
  President 1967-1974

The Mongolia Society, 1965-
  President 1967-1972
  Chairman of the Board of Directors 1967-

American Research Institute in Turkey
   Governing Board 1969-1980
   Secretary 1975-1977

Linguistic Society of America, 1954-

American Historical Association, 1964-

United Kingdom

Royal Asiatic Society of Great Britain and Ireland, 1954-
   Secretary 1955-1962

Association of British Orientalists
   Secretary 1955-1962

Philological Society, 1950-

Historical Association, 1956-

Finland

Suomalais-ugrilaisen Seura
   Honorary Fellow 1950-

France

Société asiatique, 1940-

Société de linguistique de Paris, 1940-

Germany

Deutsche Morgenländische Gesellschaft, 1958-

Hungary

Kőrösi Csoma Társaság (Hungarian Oriental Society)
   Honorary Fellow 1971-

Clubs

Cosmos Club (Washington, D.C.)
United Oxford and Cambridge University Club (London)
Explorers Club (New York)

15. HONORS, PRIZES, FELLOWSHIPS

Eduard Mahler Prize, University of Budapest, 1937

Budapest Főváros Jubiláris Ösztöndija, University of Budapest, 1937-1938

Horthy Miklós ösztöndij, University of Budapest, 1937-1938, 1938-1939

Bourse du Ministere des Affaires Étrangeres (France), 1940-1941, 1941-

Bourse de l'Association des éleves, anciens éleves et amis de l'Ecole des Langues Orientales, 1943

Elected Corresponding Member of the Suomalais-ugrilaisen Seura (Finland), 1950

Research Fellow, American Research Institute in Turkey, Istanbul, 1965

John Simon Guggenheim Fellow, 1968-1969

Elected Honorary Fellow of the Kőrösi Csoma Society (Hungary), 1971

Doctor *honoris causa*, University of Szeged (Hungary), 1971

Scholar in Residence, Rockefeller Foundation Study Center, Bellagio (Italy), 1975

Elected Honorary Member of the Hungarian Academy of Sciences, 1979

Recipient Bárczi Géza Memorial Medal for contribution to Hungarian Studies Pécs, 1981

John Simon Guggenheim Memorial Fellow, 1981-1982

Recipient Indiana University Prize for Altaic Studies (PIAC Medal), Uppsala, 1982

Recipient Arminius Vámbéry Memorial Medal for contribution to Oriental Studies, Budapest, 1983

APPENDICES

1. Biographical Sketch

Denis Sinor was born on April 17, 1916, into a Roman Catholic family of entrepreneurs in Kolozsvár, Transylvania, which at that time was still a part of Hungary. He spent his early life in Budapest, though—between the ages of ten to fifteen—for several months each year he was a pupil in the boarding school Institution Sillig in Vevey, Switzerland. Since both of his grandmothers were Austrian, he acquired a fluency in Germany almost simultaneously with Hungarian, while French governesses laid the foundation of his knowledge of their language, which was to be perfected in Vevey. At the age of ten he was duly registered in the Archiepiscopal Realgymnasium (Érseki Katholikus Reálgimnázium) in Budapest, a Roman Catholic school where the curriculum included eight years of Latin and four years of English. Contrary to appearances his education was rather unusual, since—with the exception of a few months at the age of fifteen—he never actually attended school. At the end of each academic year he passed a comprehensive examination and at the completion of the eighth year sat for the "érettségi", an examination similar in scope to the French baccalaureat. All in all, the school records reveal an average student showing no distinction in any one subject save religion in which he consistently received the best possible marks. The fact that during all these school years he had no daily obligations allowed him to read widely, in three languages and on many subjects and, in general, to lead a life remarkably free from the normal constraints placed on a school boy.

When DS was about sixteen years old his father abruptly left the world of affairs and became a gentleman farmer on a small estate near Makó, in the southeastern part of Hungary where economic and social tensions were quite strong and where the teenager came face to face with many political problems of the day. It was probably there that he acquired the deep attachment to his country of birth which, in later years, led him to so many undertakings connected with Hungary.

In 1934 DS was admitted to the Faculty of Philosophy of the University of Budapest, then called Pázmány Péter Tudományegyetem, where he was to study orientalism, more specifically the ancient Near East, the religions of which had recently captured his interest. An ukase-like order by the Turcologist Gyula Németh made him change course, and in the next few years under the direction of Németh and, in an increasing measure, under that of Lajos Ligeti, DS studied Mongol, Turcology and Inner Asian History. There are some indications that the relationship between teachers and their student was not always cloudless, but divergence of views and—one may suspect—general comportment never really soured to the point of hostility. In 1937 DS received the Mahler Award, established by Eduard Mahler of *Chronologische Tabellen* fame, to honor a promising student in oriental studies; in 1936-37 and in 1937-38 he was awarded the very generous Horthy fellowship; in 1937 he was to be the recipient of a prestigious award established by the city of Budapest to be given to *one* student chosen from among all attending the university (Budapest Székesfőváros Jubiláris Ösztöndíja). No comprehensive examination existed in fields not required of future high school teachers. Of course oriental studies belonged to this category and, at Professor Németh's suggestion, DS—in his second year and parallel with his oriental courses—took those courses required for a Hungarian-German degree. Two years later he passed the comprehensive examination (alapvizsga) with distinction in this field, though he was firmly determined never to make use of it.

Possibly because of his unusual upbringing and also, perhaps, because his family had no connections to the academic world, DS did not shy away from actions considered inappropriate in Hungarian university circles of that period. Thus, without passing through his teachers, in the summers of 1937 and 1938 he obtained permission to work in the Collegium Hungaricum in Berlin and his first two scholarly articles, published respectively in *T'oung Pao* (1937; see 3.1) and *Ostasiatische Zeitschrift* (1938; see 3.2), were never submitted—as etiquette would have required—to his teachers or to a Hungarian periodical. His stay in Berlin revealed to him the textual and artistic treasures brought there by the German Turfan expeditions and he followed gladly the suggestion of Németh and Ligeti to write his Ph.D. thesis on Turkic Buddhism. Completed in the summer of 1939, the thesis was to be defended at the end of that year in a comprehensive examination that, as it turned out, was never to take place.

Disregarding once more the usual procedure DS submitted a direct application to the Ministry for Education and with the very modest help thus obtained left for Paris. Lajos Ligeti had spent several years in Paris and had instilled in his student a respect for French civilization in general and, in particular, for that intellectual giant, Paul Pelliot. The outbreak of World War II presented DS with a difficult choice but, since Hungary was neutral in the conflict and because no authority had asked for his return, he decided to remain in Paris, facing a financially most uncertain future. The mobilization of Aurélien Sauvageot created a need for a temporary teacher of Hungarian and DS was entrusted with this task in the Ecole des Langues Orientales (ELOV). Over the course of the next three years, increasingly difficult circumstances caused by the prolongation of the war and the terrible hardships of daily life in occupied France did not dissuade DS from his efforts to absorb the teachings not only of Pelliot but also of Jean Deny, Marcel Granet and Paul Demiéville. DS is fond of recalling the long séances of Chinese readings that he had in Demiéville's unheated apartment. It is quite clear that these four scholars must have been impressed by the abilities of their young Hungarian pupil whom, with polite exaggeration, they treated as their junior colleague. As early as the spring of 1940, DS was elected a member of the Société Asiatique and of the Société de Linguistique, and the records show that as long as DS remained in France, he read a paper every year in each of these societies. Although never recalled to Hungary, support from that country was no longer forthcoming and the fellowship awarded by the French Ministry for Foreign Affairs was insufficient to provide the wherewithal of daily life particularly in view of the fact that he seemed to have little inclination for life in real poverty. In the fall of 1942 – already an assistant in Altaic studies for Pelliot at the Institut des Hautes Études Chinoises – DS was labelled "politisch unzuverlässig" and was ordered to appear in the sadly notorious offices of the German Sicherheitsdienst. At the end of a grueling interrogation, DS followed the hint of his evidently benevolent interrogator and "disappeared". For about two years he would live in clandestineness, several times being arrested by Germans and the French of Vichy, but always "talking himself free". During these clandestine years he lived mostly by selling fur coats, but found time to continue with his research. The year 1945 is the only year for which his bibliography shows no entry. He joined the Forces Françaises de l'Intérieur and, after the liberation, together with his unit, was incorporated into the Armée Rhin et Danube of Delattre de Tassigny. He was demobilized in October of 1945 from Bad Ems in Germany, a place to which he often returns.

Return to civilian life was marked by what DS considered a great personal tragedy: the death of the beloved and very influential "patron", Paul Pelliot. Some very difficult times lay ahead, but with the help of Paul Demiéville and the Indologist Louis Renou, DS was admitted to the Centre National de la Recherche Scientifique, was entrusted with some courses at the ELOV and the Institut des Hautes Études Chinoises, and by early 1948 was set for a career within the framework of French orientalism. It was not to be.

As a result of a report prepared in 1947 by Lord Scarbrough, British orientalism was to know a grandiose development. Following the initiative taken by the Sinologist Gustav Haloun, within the Faculty of Oriental Studies of Cambridge University a Lectureship in Altaic Studies was established. The post was offered to DS who, in the fall of 1948, moved to Cambridge to hold what was probably the first teaching post anywhere to carry the word "Altaic". The decision was one of great importance on the personal as well as on the professional level, but the reputation of the university and the security of a tenured position at the age of thirty-two seemed to make the choice all but inevitable. DS taught at Cambridge for thirteen full academic years. There he established the Tripos in Mongol as well as in Hungarian and taught some highly specialized courses never before – or after – offered in the old university. There is some evidence to suggest that DS's stay at Cambridge was not devoid of conflicts; these do not seem in any way to have affected his admiration for the examination system of that university and he has maintained his loyalty to Magdelene College of which he was a member. The Ph.D. examinations set by DS certainly reflect a Cantabrigian pattern.

It was during this period that DS became involved in the international organizations of orientalism in general and of Altaic studies in particular. In 1954 he was Secretary General of the 23rd Congress of Orientalists and, with the slogan "le Congrès c'est moi", established a new basis for the venerable institution and assured the presence of Altaic studies within its framework. A libretto of an "opera" written by Bernard Lewis—and actually performed at the School of Oriental and African Studies—"immortalized" DS's activities in that league. From that time until his departure from Cambridge, DS remained Honorary Secretary of the Royal Asiatic Society, was one of the secretaries (representing Great Britain) of the International Union of Orientalists, and was secretary of the Association of British Orientalists. In 1960, succeeding his good friend Walther Heissig, he became Secretary General of the Permanent International Altaistic Conference (PIAC). Several times re-elected he organized twenty-eight annual meetings and has been the principal architect of the international recognition given to that informal organization.

In the spring semester of 1962, at the suggestion of Thomas A. Sebeok, DS accepted a visiting professorship at Indiana University in the recently created Uralic and Altaic program. As he is wont to say, "a mutual love affair" developed between IU and DS who resigned his Cambridge post and moved to Bloomington—a change many found surprising. At the end of the fall semester 1962 Sebeok lost interest in the program and resigned from the chairmanship which was then offered to DS. The program, dependent only on the Graduate School of Indiana University, existed mainly on paper, the salaries of the faculty coming from a variety of departments. It is not within the scope of the present task to describe in detail the development of what was to become an unparalleled academic venture. Let it suffice that in 1967 the program became a fully fledged interdisciplinary university department within the College of Arts and Sciences and the Graduate School. At its maximum strength the department had a faculty of eighteen providing instruction in some one hundred and twenty courses with an annual enrollment in the hundreds. DS's basic idea that "offer creates the demand" was working. The strength of the department—unique in the US and probably in the world— is shown by the fact that it has continued to prosper under the chairmanship of Gustav Bayerle who took over this chore in 1981 on the retirement of DS at the age of sixty-five from Indiana University administrative posts.

In 1965 DS was asked to assume the chairmanship of the ailing Asian Studies Program of the university. He accepted the chore with some reluctance and, realizing that IU's resources were inadequate to fully maintain such a program, created the Asian Studies Research Institute (ASRI) in 1967 with a modest scope. Renamed the Research Institute for Inner Asian Studies (RIFIAS) in 1979, DS continued to serve as its director until 1981. Four years later, in 1985, DS was again called upon to assume the duties of Director of the RIFIAS. Throughout the years DS's relationship with IU's administration has been characterized by mutual respect and great cordiality. In recognition of his extraordinary services, he was given the special rank of a Distinguished Professor in 1975. Since 1963 he has been in charge, without interruption, of a federally funded Center which, since 1981, bears the name of Inner Asian and Uralic National Resource Center, the only one of its kind funded by what is today the U.S. Department of Education. Since the Center's operation has been approved for the 1985-1988 triennium, DS is expected to remain as its director beyond the age of seventy when he retires from teaching.

The brunt of DS's administrative activities in the US was focused on gaining recognition for Inner Asian studies as an independent field of scholarship and teaching activity. Thanks to his efforts in the 1970's, the Office of Education (as it was then called) recognized it as an independent "world area", and both the Association for Asian Studies and the American Oriental Society established special sections for Inner Asia. Though at one time quite active in the AAS — from 1969 to 1972 he was chairman of its International Liaison Committee — DS's sympathies lie very strongly with the more scholarly AOS. For many years he was Chairman of its Inner Asia section, and in 1975 he was honored by being elected its president. On a primarily scholarly level, DS's work on Inner Asia has brought him many special awards, including two Guggenheim Fellowships.

The present writer would not dare to sketch DS's activities in the Hungarian field. His links with Hungary have always remained very strong. In 1971 he received a Doctorate Honoris Causa from the University of Szeged and in 1981 was elected an Honorary Member of the Hungarian Academy of Sciences. IU was to derive great profit from these Hungarian connections. Beyond a steady stream of Hungarian publications reaching the library, beyond the presence in the Department of Uralic and Altaic Studies of a native instructor of Hungarian, DS achieved the extraordinary diplomatic tour de force of having the Hungarian Academy of Sciences endow a permanent chair of Hungarian Studies at IU to be a part of the Department of Uralic and Altaic Studies. He obviously derives great satisfaction from this achievement.

A latecomer to the US, his years in this country and at IU amount to more than the total spent in France and England. If, as one may suspect, it was his ambition to become what the French orientalists call a "grand mandarin", he must feel that he has fulfilled this. IU, Inner Asian, and Uralic and Altaic scholarship have all seen the benefits of this aim thus achieved. Multi-lingual, multi- or rather supra-national and apolitical, DS has been a constant and efficient link between scholars working under different and often opposed political systems. He has been welcome in the USSR and the PRC as well as in Taiwan and South Korea, in West as well as in East Germany, totally impervious to political or ideological biases. In a long life DS has served, and served well, four countries and international scholarship.

Indiana University   RUTH I. MESERVE

2. Denis Sinor at Indiana University

It was in the fall of 1962 that Thomas A. Sebeok, director of the Uralic and Altaic Studies Program, brought Denis Sinor, a Cambridge don for the previous sixteen years, to Indiana University. Within a year's time he became chair of the program (now a regular academic department), a post which he relinquished on his sixty-fifth birthday in the Spring of 1981. In 1965 he succeeded Joseph L. Sutton as chair of the Asian Studies Program. Within another two years he became Director of the Asian Studies Research Center, but in 1979, after the Center had dropped Korean Studies in favor of Tibetan Studies, it was renamed the Research Institute for Inner Asian Studies in order to more correctly identify its true focus. Professor Sinor relinquished this post also in 1981. He still holds, however, the post of Director (to which he was also appointed in 1963) of the NDEA Uralic and Inner Asian Language and Area Center, renamed in 1981 as the Inner Asian and Uralic National Resource Center.

The Uralic and Altaic Studies Department at Indiana University is unique among American institutions. In fact, there is no other academic unit quite like it in higher learning anywhere else in the world. Much of its success is due to the reputation of its esteemed faculty, most of whom were hired by Professor Sinor. It has also profited greatly from the symbiotic relationship it has had, under a common chair or director, with the Inner Asian and Uralic National Resource Center. The IAUNRC is one of four (formerly six) national area centers at Indiana University funded by the U.S. Department of Education, but it is the only Inner Asian Center in the entire United States. As a result of the Center's support, the Uralic and Altaic Studies Department is able to teach a large number of foreign languages on a regular basis. These include: Hungarian, Finnish, Turkish, Classical and Modern Mongolian, Tibetan, Estonian, Uzbek and Azeri. Those occasionally taught include: Manchu, Tatar, Chuvash, Yakut, Tuvin, Old Turkic, Cheremis, Mordvin. It would be difficult to find this cluster of language instruction at any other university.

From the very beginning of his nearly a quarter of a century at Indiana University, Professor Sinor has taught a large number and a large variety of courses in the Uralic and Altaic Studies Department. Altogether, it amounts to nearly thirty different courses. They range from broad undergraduate survey courses to specialized graduate topics, colloquia, and seminar courses. They include civilization courses as well as special language courses. The languages he has taught include Manchu, and Classical Mongolian, but, above all, he has taught Hungarian at practically every level from the first to the fourth year. Probably no one else in the department can match this diversity in student course offerings.

Professor Sinor has also held a joint appointment in the Department of History for nearly as long as he has been here. For years his two courses in the history of Hungary and his two courses on the history of the Mongols were regular offerings on an overload basis, giving additional support to History's already strong emphasis on Eastern Europe and Asian history. But he did much more than just teach; he served on departmental committees and regularly attended faculty meetings, especially those dealing with hiring, promotion, and tenure. In many ways he pulled his oar even though many members did not know that he was not on the History budget. Although he had helped make modern history as a member of the French Resistance Movement during World War II, his own interests lay within the medieval period, and the History Department counted on him to give strength not only in medieval Eastern Europe but Inner Asia as well. A continuing testimony to his historical expertise in the latter area is his very successful career as founder and sole editor of the *Journal of Asian History* for the past twenty years.

In addition to the Uralic and Altaic Studies Department's two distinguished professorships, that of Denis Sinor and Tom Sebeok, it has had a Chair of Hungarian Studies ever since January, 1981. Conceived as a possibility by Professor Sinor, he convinced both John W. Ryan, President of Indiana University, and Ferenc Marta, Secretary General of the Hungarian Academy of Sciences, that it was worthy of implementation. The agreement to establish such a chair of Hungarian Studies at Indiana University was signed on 15 June 1979 by Béla Köpeczi for the Hungarian Academy of Sciences and by President Ryan. The first holder of the chair is György Ránki (January, 1981-1987), whose vigorous energy has resulted in many activities and conferences that have enriched the life of the University. President Ryan's unstinting support of this project stems from his vision for strong international studies programs at I.U., much in the tradition of Chancellor Herman B Wells.

Although Professor Sinor's personal life has not been without its tragic aspects, and although he has encountered difficulties with his health (sometimes in far-off places and climes), his gracious manner and bearing carry much old world charm. He is a man who respects the Shakespearean hierarchies of "degree, order, and place," who administers his various worlds without a great deal of respect for the niceties of university self-governance but with a great deal of respect for academic quality and excellence. He has been seen on some occasions dangerously driving his motor scooter across miles of crowded highway and at other times he has hardly been able to put one foot ahead of the next as he labored to walk across the campus. His annual parties for his colleagues and friends were a social highlight of the fall semester, and his family's gracious hospitality is unmatched in the city of Bloomington. His cheery greeting always lifts one's spirits.

For one untutored in the ways a major American research university operates, Professor Sinor learned quickly how to become a skilled administrator. His successful negotiations with the Department of Education each year, his creation of the Hungarian chair, and even his establishment of the Indiana University annual prize to a distinguished Altaic Studies scholar—as part of his position for nearly thirty years as the Secretary General of the Permanent

International Altaistic Conference—all testify to his initiative and enterprise in publicizing—indeed developing—Altaic Studies. Nothing was more characteristic of Denis Sinor, with tongue in cheek, than his frequent opening remark to a small group of friends: "What have you done for me lately?" What one may not realize until later in such an off-guard situation is that here is a man who has already given so much of himself to the University that it is grateful he forsook the old world for the new even though his heart also remains in Hungary and Inner Asia.

Indiana University   LEO F. SOLT
                                                    Professor of History and
                                                    Dean of the Graduate School

3. La Contribution de Denis Sinor aux Études Médiévales

La notion même de Moyen Age a été définie à partir de phénomènes qui sont propres à l'Europe, et les limites chronologiques qui ont été imposées à ce millénaire de l'histoire du monde se réfèrent à l'effacement de l'empire romain d'Occident, d'une part, à la chute de l'empire romain d'Orient, à l'avènement de la Renaissance et à l'ouverture des routes maritimes à l'expansion européenne, de l'autre. C'est-à-dire à des mutations qui affectent essentiellement l'histoire de l'Europe et du bassin méditerranéen.

Et cependant cette histoire est inséparable de celle du vaste continent eurasiatique. L'Europe, certes, n'est pas seulement un cap de l'Eurasie; mais les transformations qui l'ont affectée à travers les âges ont bien souvent pris naissance quelque part dans ce que René Grousset a défini, d'un mot heureux, comme "l'empire des steppes". Et le médiéviste, qui mène ses recherches à l'aide de méthodes définies par rapport à l'histoire du Moyen Age européen, attend beaucoup, parfois sans s'en rendre compte, de ce que l'on découvre du passé de ce monde qui s'étend entre l'Extrême-Orient et les pays du Danube.

Lorsque le nom de Denis Sinor est apparu pour la première fois au bas d'une étude destinée à marquer dans les cercles médiévistes, c'était précisément à propos de l'une de ces interventions des peuples de l'Eurasie intérieure aux frontières de l'Occident européen. Ouverte par l'apparition des Huns sur les arrières des peuples gothiques, la période des *Völkerwanderungen* ne s'est en effet arrêtée que par la destruction de l'empire des Avars, réalisée par Charlemagne, et par l'enracinement des Hongrois dans la plaine pannonienne. L'article que publia en 1946-1947 le *Journal Asiatique* sous le titre "Autour d'une migration de peuples au Ve siècle" (3.12) reprenait dans son ensemble l'histoire de ces peuples mal identifiés et connus par des sources totalement indépendantes les unes des autres que sont les Avars, les Onogours, les Sabirs, les Hongrois eux-mêmes. D. Sinor prenait en considération les historiens grecs, Kašgari, les données chinoises, les leçons de la linguistique, celles de la mythologie et de l'ethnologie pour jeter bas nombre d'hypothèses dont il démontrait la fragilité, et pour inviter les historiens à chercher dans la zone comprise entre l'Oural et le Caucase le point de départ de l'ébranlement de peuples appelés à s'adjoindre les éléments d'autres groupes ethniques pour former ces vagues d'invasions dont on allait parfois chercher la source bien loin, jusqu'à l'Est de la Sibérie. Il amenait ainsi les historiens du Haut Moyen Age à revoir leurs synthèses.

De cette période ancienne, il ne pouvait manquer de passer à la grande époque des contacts entre l'Occident et les peuples des steppes: le XIIIe siècle. D'abord avant l'établissement de la domination mongole: dans "Quelques passages relatifs aux Comans tirés des chroniques françaises de l'époque des Croisades" (3.31), il attirait l'attention sur un aspect négligé de l'histoire de l'empire latin de Constantinople, celui des relations nouées entre les Latins et les Qipčaq. Ceux-ci, d'abord regardés comme des auxiliaires du tsar des Bulgares, devinrent des alliés, surtout lorsque telles de leurs hordes, fuyant l'avance mongole, cherchèrent accueil auprès des Francs de Constantinople avec lesquels certains de leurs chefs nouèrent des alliances matrimoniales. Parallèlement, les missionnaires hongrois qui travaillaient à l'évangélisation des mêmes Comans allaient se mettre à la recherche du rameau du peuple hongrois que l'on disait être resté dans son habitat primitif. Dans un important article sur "Un voyageur du XIIIe siècle: le Dominicain Julien de Hongrie" (3.24), D. Sinor cherchait à déterminer la part de réalité et la part d'affabulation que contenait la relation du voyage des quatre Dominicains qui partirent pour cette expédition, telle que nous l'a conservée la chronique de Riccardo de San-Germano.

Avec Julien de Hongrie parvenaient en Europe les premières informations sur l'approche de la grande armée mongole qui dévastait en 1240-1241 la Pologne, la Bohême et la Hongrie. L'inquiétude ressentie en Occident provoquait l'envoi d'ambassades auprès des envahisseurs. D. Sinor a spécialement étudié la tradition textuelle du récit de Plancarpin ("John of Plano Carpini's return from the Mongols. New Light from a Luxemburg manuscript"; 3.25), et les vocables figurant dans ce récit et provenant des langues turque et mongole ("Mongol and Turkic words in the Latin versions of John of Plano Carpini's *Journey to the Mongols*"; 3.59), de même qu'il a étudié une expression figurant dans une lettre d'un khan à un roi de France ("The mysterious Talu Sea in Öljeitü's letter to Philip the Fair"; 3.64). En ces dernières années, c'est aux indispensables drogmans qui rendaient possibles les échanges à l'intérieur du monde mongol qu'il s'est attaché (par exemple, dans "Interpreters in medieval Inner Asia"; 3.94).

Ces études portant sur des points particuliers débouchent sur deux gros articles de synthèse ("Les relations entre les Mongols et l'Europe jusqu'à la mort d'Arghoun et de Bela IV" 3.32; "Le Mongol vu par l'Occident; 3.82) qui nous apportent une vue très complète et souvent personnelle de ce que furent les contacts belliqueux ou pacifiques entre les Gengiskhanides et les

Occidentaux, et les limites de la compréhension entre les uns et les autres. Et aussi un gros chapitre de l'*History of the Crusades* sur le même sujet.

On ne s'étonnera donc pas que le volume des *Variorum Reprints* qui, en 1977, a rassemblé l'essentiel de ces travaux ait pris pour titre *Inner Asia and its contacts with medieval Europe* (1.5). La contribution de Denis Sinor apparaît centrée ici sur ces contacts, ces relations, sur lesquels sa profonde connaissance de l'Asie intérieure, de ses langues, de ses traits de civilisation, lui permettaient de jeter une lumière nouvelle.

Mais là ne se limite pas ce qu'il a apporté à nos études. N'oublions pas les articles donnés notamment à l'*Encyclopaedia britannica* et à la *New Catholic Encyclopedia,* traitant d'histoire hongroise comme d'histoire de l'Asie intérieure et surtout mongole. Ni les très nombreuses recensions et les comptes-rendus qu'il a dispensés dans divers périodiques, et tout particulièrement dans ce *Journal of Asian History* qui a apporté aux historiens ayant à se référer à l'histoire de l'Asie un outil de travail spécialement adapté à leurs besoins. Il n'est d'étude parue dans le domaine que nous avons envisagé dont il n'ait rendu compte, signalant les centres d'intérêt, corrigeant certaines données, donnant son propre point de vue. Et, si ces comptes-rendus peuvent apparaître comme alimentant une bibliographie courante, l'*Introduction à l'étude de l'Eurasie centrale* (1.3) fournit l'ouvrage fondamental, l'instrument de travail dont les médiévistes ne sont pas les seuls à apprécier l'utilité, mais qui leur permet de ne plus se considérer comme exclus des espaces peuplés par ceux qui parlent une langue finno-ougrienne, turque, mongole, tibétaine, et, à l'inverse, d'exclure par principe de leur horizon le vaste monde des steppes!

Qu'il soit permis d'ajouter qu'en créant et en animant la Permanent International Altaistic Conference, D. Sinor a complété cette oeuvre en facilitant les contacts entre tels médiévistes (et le signataire de ces lignes est de ceux-là) et les spécialistes des domaines linguistiques et ehtnographiques de l'Asie intérieure, pour la meilleure information, peut-être, des uns et des autres.

Denis Sinor est de ceux qui savent ce que nous devons tous à nos précurseurs. Non seulement pour leur rendre l'hommage qu'ils méritent, mais aussi pour garder à leurs oeuvres leur caractère d'ouvrages fondamentaux et toujours utiles. Il a, par exemple, traduit *Le Conquérant du Monde* (9.10) de René Grousset, parmi d'autres. Aussi pensons-nous qu'il ne serait pas pour lui d'éloge plus apprécié que de lui appliquer de que l'on peut dire de son maître Paul Pelliot, qui reste pour les orientalistes un des plus grands noms parmi les savants qui ont illustré leurs disciplines; mais qui, pour les médiévistes de stricte observance, demeure aussi l'un des leurs. De ceux qui manient avec maîtrise les techniques de l'érudition, de la chronologie comme de la critique des textes, en même temps qu'ils sont à même d'ouvrir à leurs émules les vastes perspectives du continent eurasiatique. Denis Sinor, lui aussi, pratique l'art du médiéviste comme il joue du clavier des langues orientales, et c'est ce qui lui a permis d'ouvrir des voies nouvelles à l'histoire du Moyen Age.

Dijon, France   JEAN RICHARD

4. Denis Sinor and Uralic Studies

According to a Hungarian anecdote a literary scholar used to write science articles for other people in order to make some money in his student years. No one knows if this was really true but the message is obvious: if need be, a well trained philologist can use his scholarly talents in fields distant from his own. This story could easily be true of Denis Sinor as well. His diverse scholarly work is grounded on a systematic training in philology, a wide knowledge of the sources and his ability to unearth them, a respect for facts, the identification and a particular way of presenting problems. Rather than offer plausible final solutions, Sinor often makes the reader think through problems and lets him choose a solution from several alternatives.

Denis Sinor's work in Uralic Studies is characterized by the same scholarly attributes as are seen in his non-Uralic work. Although he has no degree in Uralic Studies and cannot be regarded as a professional Uralist, he has often had to deal with this research field. He has not made any strictly Uralic "discoveries", that is, he has not written any syntheses or monographs on a Uralic language or on Uralic reconstructions. His contribution to Uralic Studies is of a different kind. He evaluates the findings of Uralic (or other) studies from his own point of view and in doing so he uses Si-norm (< Sinor + norm), for which he has been criticized by professional Finno-Ugrists in a few cases (e.g. *UAJb* 41.300). However, he has been playing the devil's advocate consciously.

I believe it is a truism that DS is not a linguist; indeed, he considers himself to be a historian. This scholarly attitude is manifest also in his Uralic work. In his publications he first of all presents a legion of (linguistic) facts, on the basis of which he poses the problem, and, whenever necessary, provides a wide historical-cultural background. He gives his opinion, sometimes partly skeptically, never forcing the reader to accept it. He is brave enough to believe and not believe at the same time. He can see the puzzles; their solution is not always clear to him, which he tells his readers because he is all too well aware of the shocking surprises scholarship holds in store for students. The oft-mentioned nonconclusive character of his conclusions is perhaps due to his sceptical personality and his awareness of potential miscalculations in scholarship. This is how I have known DS as a Uralist colleague and I believe his work outside Uralic Studies shows similar characteristics.

Denis Sinor has been active in a wide range of Uralic Studies. The history of Uralic languages has been one of his favorite fields; his "excursions" into comparative Uralic linguistics have always been motivated by his interest in Altaic languages. From the beginning he has been interested in the so-called Uralic-Altaic hypothesis, a highly controversial matter which he would like to clarify. The Ural-Altaic hypothesis is actually so controversial that one should be extremely careful about its examination. As time has passed, Sinor has offered increasingly more subtle answers to the problem. Such a development

50 APPENDICES

in a scholar's work is inevitable if he keeps up with the new results in his
field. His papers using Uralic linguistic data bear witness to his knowledge
of sources and his ability to use them. He has continually and systematically
followed the Uralic literature, noting all the new and important works. In his
"D'un morphème particulièrement répandu dans les langues ouralo-altaïques"
(*TP* 1943, see 3.8) he examined the locative suffix *-n* in the Turkic and Uralic
languages. This paper relied on the somewhat outdated yet classical manuals
by J. SZINNYEI (*Magyar nyelvhasonlítás*, 7th impression, 1927 and *Finnisch-
ugrische Sprachwissenschaft*, 2nd impression, Berlin, 1922). However, in a
paper published nine years later ("On some Uralic-Altaic plural suffixes",
Asia Major NS 2, 1952, see 3.23) Sinor already cited the work of M. A.
CASTRÉN, A. AHLQVIST, Y. WICHMANN, T. E. UOTILA, J. MARK, Ö. BEKE,
H. PAASONEN, the then modern L. HAKULINEN, and P. RAVILA – all of them
major sources to this date.

The above two papers and a number of others (e.g. "Az uráli – mandzsu-
tunguz kapcsolatokhoz", *Magyar Nyelv* 1950, see 3.19; "Le Problème de la
parenté des langues ouralo-altaïques", *Revue de GHE* 1948, see 3.15;
"Ouralo-altaïque – Indo-européen", *TP* 1944, see 3.11; "Uralic and Altaic: the
neglected area", 1964, see 3.49; "Geschichtliche Hypothesen und Sprachwissenschaft in der ungarischen finnisch-ugrischen und uralischen Sprachwissenschaft", *UAJb* 1969, see 3.51; "Altaica and Uralica" in *Studies in Finno-
Ugric Linguistics in honor of Alo Raun*, 1977, see 3.80; and "Az urál-altaji
nyelvrokonság problémája", see 10.172, a paper read at the Congressus
Sextus Internationalis Fenno-Ugristarum in Syktyvkar on July 26, 1985) show
Sinor's interest in the correspondences between the Uralic and Altaic language
families. As I said above, Sinor's solution (or shall I call it, more modestly,
his approach?) has been gradually modified all along. As a young scholar he
thought that the correspondences between Uralic and Altaic languages were
not accidental yet the genetic relatedness of these languages could not be
proved. Sinor the Altaic scholar was well aware of the difficulties of problems
with respect to the genetic relationship of the languages within the Altaic
family, and, if nothing else, this alone made him cautious. He went as far as
proposing "an undeniably close link" between the Uralic and Altaic languages
on the basis of certain suffixes. Of course, he emphasized the fact that the
similar suffixes in question are not used the same way even within the Altaic
language family, cf., e.g., the great variety of the plural suffixes in Mongolian.
The linguistic explanation of some contradictory phenomena is therefore
sometimes vague, the vagueness of Sinor's explanations is partly due to his
research intentions, partly to the problems he investigates.

In his later work DS attempted to pose the problems of the Uralic-Altaic
hypothesis against a somewhat clearer background. He was undeniably right
in showing that the genetic relatedness of Uralic and Turkic (Altaic) grammatical
morphemes could not be explained by the traditional methods of comparative
linguistics (cf. "A Ural-Altaic ordinal suffix", *UAJb* 1959, see 3.38 and

"Un suffixe de lieu ouralo-altaïque", *AOH*, 1961, see 3.40). Some scholars have gone along with Sinor on this problem. He claimed that the correspondences go back to prehistoric times when language mixture and borrowing played highly complex roles in the complicated ethnogenetic development of the Eurasian peoples. This position brings DS near to a looser, non-dogmatic explanation of the Uralic and Altaic protolanguages. Although unusual, his approach yields a new grouping of Uralic and Altaic languages; one which considers geographic factors in the shaping of languages during the whirligig of peoples and tongues. In this connection DS called attention to the possibility of more numerous correspondences between Uralic and Turkic or Tungus than, for instance, between Uralic and Mongolian, although he does not deny the possibility of the latter correspondences either (cf. "Urine – star – nail", *MSFOu* 72, 1973, see 3.66). In his famous "Uralo-Tunguz lexical correspondences" (*BOH* 20, 1975, see 3.72) DS proposed 37 correspondences on the basis of the recent historical phonological and etymological literature. He offers several possible explanations for the etymological correspondences between Uralic and Tungus: perhaps Finno-Ugric and Tungus were in contact at one time, perhaps they both borrowed words from a third language. . . .

It is here that Sinor constructs a new, geography-based model of the interrelationship of Uralic and Altaic languages. His model brings the areal discussion and interpretation of the Ural-Altaic hypothesis into focus. The essence of the model is this: the linguistic correspondences are due to the geographic connections between the language groups which formed a circle, with Samoyed in the north, Tungus to the east of Samoyed, Mongolian to the south of Tungus, Turkic to the east of Mongolian, and Finno-Ugric between Turkic and Samoyed. The interrelationships among these groups are rather complicated and will probably be the subject of further research.

DS has written a state of the art paper ("The Present State of Uralic and Altaic Comparative Studies", Seoul, 1975, see 3.76) which testifies to his persistent attention to Uralic studies and his use of the results in his own work. In this paper he quite unequivocally states that there is no protolanguage to which the Uralic and Altaic correspondences could go back. The correspondences are areal, whose isoglosses sometimes go from Indo-European to Inner Asia, thus creating the impression of genetic correspondences. This view is fairly close to one trend in today's Uralic linguistics. His "The $*-t \sim *-d$ local suffix in Uralic and Altaic" (*Hungaro-Turcica* 1975, see 3.78) pursues the same topic and argues against a simplistic, yes-or-no approach to the study of the genetic relationship of languages. He is right in his assertion that scholars must know the facts about Uralic and Altaic languages before attempting to explain them. DS's main concern is to learn the facts and to make them known to others. First of all, facts should be unearthed; their explanation can be done later.

Sinor's eagerness to find facts is manifest in his "The Nature of Possessive Suffixes in Uralic and Altaic" (*Hill-Festschrift*, 1978, see 3.85) and his

"Samoyed and Ugric Elements in Old Turkic" (*Pritsak-Festschrift*, 1979-1980, see 3.87). The latter paper is the re-opening of an old case, a worthy piece of work, even if I do not agree with the historical proof of the contacts which is based on the ethnonym *Mančud* in the Tonyuquq inscription as read by G. J. RAMSTEDT and P. AALTO, and on I. VÁSÁRY's etymology according to which the Turkic river name *Käm* 'Yenisei' goes back to Samoyed. In spite of this Sinor's etymologies deserve the attention of students of Hungarian, Ugric, Samoyed and Turkic.

In reading Sinor's Altaistic papers one will almost always come upon remarks that are relevant to the study of Hungarian (Finno-Ugric) prehistory or linguistics. In "Qapqan" (*JRAS* 1954, see 3.30), for instance, he remarks on the Hungarian name *Koppány.* And who would have expected him to deal with the Hungarian word *ló* 'horse', moreover, Ugric horse-breeding, in "Notes on the equine terminology of the Altaic people" (*CAJ* 1965, see 3.50).

If I were to survey all the Uralic and Hungarian references in Sinor's *par excellence* Altaistic work, I would need several more pages. Instead, let me mention in passing the large volume of his reviews. They bear witness to DS's excellent ability to pick and choose from the large corpus of Uralic and Hungarian studies. He has informed his western colleagues of most major works in these fields, often acclaiming achievements, but not sparing criticism if need be.

A sizeable portion of DS's scholarly output bears directly on Hungarian prehistory: "The Outlines of Hungarian Prehistory" (1958, see 3.36), "Les relations entre les Mongols et l'Europe jusqu'à la mort d'Arghoun et de Béla IV" (1956, see 3.32), "Central Eruasia" (1954, see 2.1), "Inner Asia—Central Eurasia" (1974, see 3.70), and "The Mongols and Western Europe" (1975, see 3.74).

Some of his papers are about teaching Hungarian language and culture (or "teaching Hungary" as he would call it) to Americans. He has written articles on major figures in Hungarian literature for several prestigious encyclopedias, which might not be the peaks of his scholarly activity but have certainly helped make Hungary and Hungarians better known in the western hemisphere. His *History of Hungary* (1st edition 1959, see 1.2) has done an equally good service in this respect.

Inner Asia: History—Civilization—Languages (1969, see 1.4), *Introduction à l'étude de l'Eurasie Centrale* (1963, see 1.3) and *Inner Asia and its Contacts with Medieval Europe* (1977, see 1.5), are reference books that Sinor has packed full of useful information on Uralic languages and peoples. DS has edited *Studies in Finno-Ugric Linguistics in Honor of Alo Raun* (1977, see 2.8), *Modern Hungary* (1977, see 2.9), an anthology from the New Hungarian Quarterly, he has compiled a short Hungarian-English dictionary (1956, see 1.1) and has initiated the preparation of *A Handbook of Uralic Studies.* Volume 1 (see 2.10) of the latter title will probably be published by the time this bibliography appears. A selection of his papers containing articles directly relevant to Hungarian linguists but not easily available in Hungary has been published in Hungarian (*Tanulmányok*, 1982, see 1.6).

Denis Sinor is a globe-trotter and he frequently comes to Hungary. When in his native land, he often wears the hat of the vice-president of the International Association of Hungarian Studies, or the one of the chairman of the editorial board of the Association's journal *Hungarian Studies*. He participates in the work of *Anyanyelvi Konferencia,* a "movement" to foster the Hungarian language beyond the borders of Hungary. Often interviewed on radio and television and in the papers, he is a "media person", a "public figure", a V.I.P. in Budapest whose witty remarks frequently surprise viewers, listeners, readers and journalists alike in his beloved home country. How well known he is in Hungary became clear to me when a few years ago we had lunch at *Vörös Sün,* a restaurant on the Castle Hill in Buda. Denis had been on Hungarian television a few days earlier and the chef of *Vörös Sün* recognized him. I consider that quite a spectacular success for a philologist. He received the best meal *Vörös Sün* has ever produced and, on top of that, he was served a large glass of water full of ice (DS is the only Hungarian in Hungary who drinks such a beverage).

Budapest, Hungary   PÉTER HAJDÚ
                                          Chairman of the Section
                                          Language and Literature of the
                                          Hungarian Academy of Sciences

5. Denis Sinor und die Mandschustudien

Denis Sinors "mandschurische Bibliographie" beginnt mit dem Artikel *La transcription du Mandjou* (in *Journal Asiatique,* Nr. 237 [1949], S. 261-272, s. 3.16), das heißt mit einem Problem, das auf Grund des Schicksals des Mandschuvolkes auch heute noch das Interesse der Sprachwissenschaftler erweckt. Auch heute noch wird die Diskussion über die Umschrift des mandschurischen Alphabets fortgesetzt, obgleich sich inzwischen zwei Systeme allgemein durchgesetzt haben—in Europa das *von Gabelentz—Hauer*'sche System, in Übersee das *von Möllendorff*'sche. Beide Systeme sind nicht frei von Unklarheiten, unterscheiden nicht immer zwischen Transkription und Transliteration. Sinor hat mit seinem Vier-Punkte-Postulat (S. 263) in bezug auf eine allgemein akzeptable Umschrift einen bedeutenden Beitrag auf diesem Gebiet geleistet; seine Überlegungen wurden von der "ungarischen" Schule weiterentwickelt—man vergleiche den Artikel von L. LIGETI, *A propos de l'écriture mandchoue* (in *AOH* 2/1952, S. 235-299)—und wenn heute die in Ungarn verwendete Umschrift des Mandschurischen als die exakteste bezeichnet werden kann, so ist dies wohl auch ein Verdienst von Denis Sinor und seinen Vorarbeiten. Im selben Jahr veröffentlichte Sinor auch seine Arbeit *Le verbe mandjou* (in *Bulletin de la Société de linguistique de Paris*, 45/I, n° 13 [1949], S. 146-155; s. 3.17), wohl mit der Absicht, klare Grenzen in dem so unübersichtlichen Gebiet wie dem des mandschurischen "Verbes" zu schaffen.

1954 folgte seine *Introduction aux études mandjoues* (in *T'oung Pao* 42 [1954], S. 70-100; s. 3.27), die Sinor folgendermaßen definierte: "un échantillon, modifié, d'un travail qui portera le titre 'Introduction à l'étude du l'Eurasie Centrale'" (S. 71, s. 1.3). Letzteres wurde 1963 bei O. Harrassowitz in Wiesbaden veröffentlicht und ist inzwischen zu einem Klassiker der ural-altaischen Studien geworden, in dem die Bibliographie zu den Mandschustudien in eine sprachwissenschaftliche (S. 161-174) und in eine geschichtliche Sektion (S. 336-337) eingeteilt wurde. Dieses auch heute noch unübertroffene Werk stellt den ersten Versuch dar, in einer einzigen Bibliographie neben Werken in westlichen Sprachen auch solche in russischer und japanischer Sprache aufzunehmen.

1958 verfaßte Sinor eine ausführliche Beschreibung der mandschurischen Sprache (*La langue mandjoue*, in *Handbuch der Orientalistik, Erste Abteilung: Der Nahe und der Mittlere Osten, fünfter Band: Altaistik, dritter Abschnitt: Tungusologie*, S. 257-280; s. 3.56), die 1968 von E. J. Brill (Leiden-Köln) veröffentlicht wurde.

Genau zehn Jahre später veröffentlichte Sinor jene Arbeit, die auf die zukünftigen Studien auf dem Gebiet der mandschurischen Literatur einen entscheidenden Einfluß ausübte: es handelte sich um seine *Some Remarks on Manchu Poetry* (in *Studies in South, East, and Central Asia Presented as a Memorial Volume to the Late Professor Raghu Vira by Members of the Permanent International Altaistic Conference*, New Delhi 1968, S. 105-114; s. 3.54). Dieser Artikel stellt die erste Analyse der mandschurischen Verstechnik dar, deren Existenz fast zwei Jahrhunderte lang verneint und erst seit der Mitte unseres Jahrhunderts akzeptiert wurde — und zwar nur in Bezug auf den Stabreim. Sinor analysiert hier einige dichterische Passagen der "Mongolischen Chronik" von Saghang Sechen, die viersprachige Inschrift von 1765 zur Restaurierung des Tempels *An-yüan-miao* in Jehol sowie die Anrufungen der Schamanen-Erzählung *Nišan saman-i bithe*. Zum ersten Mal werden hier Begriffe wie Vierzeiler, Zäsur, feststehende Silben- und Wortzahl, Reimschema u.s.w. verwendet, wodurch Sinor den Beweis erbrachte, daß auch die mandschurische Poesie genau festgesetzten und raffiniert ausgearbeiteten Versregeln unterworfen war. Spätere Forschungen haben ergeben, daß Sinors Schlußfolgerungen in jeder Beziehung den Tatsachen entsprachen, als er schrieb: ". . . there was an indigenous Manchu poetry and. . . the consciousness of the poetic possibilities of the language was vivid enough for translators to attempt the rendering into Manchu of sophisticated, foreign metrical structures" (S. 114).

Nach dieser Arbeit über die Mandschu-Poetik widmete sich Sinor der mandschurischen Literatur im allgemeinen und veröffentlichte in italienischer Sprache den Beitrag *I fondamenti della letteratura mancese* (in *Le letterature del mondo, vol. IV: Storia delle letterature d'Oriente*, Milano 1969, S. 383-411;

s. 3.58). Ein schwieriges, bis dahin noch nie versuchtes Unternehmen: alle bisherigen mandschurischen Literaturgeschichten (von B. LAUFER, A. V. GREBENŠČIKOV, W. FUCHS) sind meistens nur trockene Aufzählungen von Buchtiteln und gehen nicht näher und kritisch auf den Inhalt der einzelnen Werke ein.

Diese Arbeit beginnt mit einer kurzen geschichtlichen Einleitung (S. 383-385) und erklärt anschließend dem Leser die Eigenheiten der mandschurischen Sprache (S. 386-388). Daran schließen sich einige Überlegungen über die orale Literatur an, mit denen Sinor mit einem Vorsprung von fast zwanzig Jahren die reiche, erst kürzlich zugängliche orale Literatur der Mandschuren hervorhebt.

Auf. S. 389 schlägt Sinor dann folgende Einteilung der mandschurischen Literatur in vier Perioden vor:

1) Antikes Zeitalter (bis 1664, d.h. bis zur Veröffentlichung des *Hafu buleku bithe*);
2) Goldenes Zeitalter (die *K'ang-hsi*-Periode);
3) Silbernes Zeitalter (die *Ch'ien-lung*-Periode);
4) Zeitalter der Dekadenz (19. Jahrhundert).

Die ganze Literatur wird sodann "nach Argumenten und Genres" unterteilt, um "eine einfache geschichtliche Aufzählung der zur Verfügung stehenden Texte" zu verhindern (S. 389). Die mandschurischen Werke sind daher in die Abschnitte "schöngeistige Literatur," "historische Literatur", "linguistische Literatur", "politische Literatur" und "religiöse Literatur" eingeteilt. In der "historischen Literatur" setzt Sinor seine Analyse der Mandschu-Poetik fort und wirft sein Augemerk auf Steininschriften, auf Saghang Sechen's Chronik und auf das *Nišan saman-i bithe*.

Diese neue, heute allgemein akzeptierte Vision der mandschurischen Literatur, und vor allem seine Studien über die mandschurische Vers-Technik rechtfertigen es, Denis Sinor einen Ehrenplatz unter den westlichen "Mandschuristen" einzuräumen. Man kann, ganz objektiv betrachtet, behaupten, daß die gegenwärtig durchgeführten Studien auf dem Gebiet der Mandschu-Poetik durch Sinors Forschungsarbeit angeregt wurden. Wenn heutzutage das Studium dieser Poetik fast tagtäglich neue Erkenntnisse zu Tage bringt, so ist dies auch—oder vor allem—ein Verdienst von Denis Sinor, der als erster die Geheimnisse der mandschurischen Dichtkunst erkennt und allgemein zugänglich gemacht hat.

Venice University / Italy   GIOVANNI STARY

TABULA GRATULATORIA

The American Oriental Society
New Haven, Connecticut

BORIS ARAPOVIC
Stockholm, Sweden

JES P. ASMUSSEN
Copenhagen, Denmark

FRANÇOISE AUBIN
Beaufort-en-Vallée, France

ROBERT AUSTERLITZ
New York, New York

GRACE BAREIKIS
Bloomington, Indiana

ROBERT P. BAREIKIS
Bloomington, Indiana

ILHAN BAŞGÖZ
Bloomington, Indiana

N. A. BASKAKOV
Moscow, USSR

HAROLD R. BATTERSBY
Geneseo, New York

CHARLES BAWDEN
Iver, England

GUSTAV BAYERLE
Bloomington, Indiana

CHRISTOPHER I. BECKWITH
Bloomington, Indiana

GIAMPIERO BELLINGERI
Venezia, Italy

ERNEST BENDER
Philadelphia, Pennsylvania

MARIANNA D. BIRNBAUM
Los Angeles, California

DERK BODDE
Philadelphia, Pennsylvania

A. J. E. BODROGLIGETI
Los Angeles, California

C. R. BOXER
Little Gaddesden, England

MARY BOYCE
London, England

YURI BREGEL
Bloomington, Indiana

BERNT BRENDEMOEN
Oslo, Norway

BESS ANN BROWN
Munich, Federal Republic
of Germany

ZIYA M. BUNIYATOV
Baku, USSR

LYNTON KEITH CALDWELL
Bloomington, Indiana

ALICIA J. CAMPI
Tokyo, Japan

CHARLES F. CARLSON
Munich, Federal Republic
of Germany

LOKESH CHANDRA
New Delhi, India

CHIEH-HSIEN CH'EN
Taipei, Taiwan, Republic of China

CHING-LUNG CHEN
Taipei, Taiwan, Republic of China

OU-YANG CHIH
Taipei, Taiwan, Republic of China

ELISABETTA CHIODO
Roma, Italy

ARISTA MARIE CIRTAUTAS
Seattle, Washington

JOHN GORDON COATES
Cambridge, England

FRANCES COOLEY
Cambridge, England

NICOLA DI COSMO
Venezia, Italy

PAOLO DAFFINA
Roma, Italy

GYULA DÉCSY
Bloomington, Indiana

LINDA DÉGH
Bloomington, Indiana

ALBERT E. DIEN
Stanford, California

LUCIANO DORINI
Roma, Italy

RICHARD W. DORN
Wiesbaden, Federal Republic
of Germany

MARK J. DRESDEN
Media, Pennsylvania

STEPHEN DURRANT
Salt Lake City, Utah

WOLFRAM EBERHARD
Berkeley, California

AINSLIE T. EMBREE
New York, New York

EUGENE C. EOYANG
Bloomington, Indiana

MARCEL ERDAL
Mount Scopus, Jerusalem

J. RUFUS FEARS
Bloomington, Indiana

HENRY A. FISCHEL
Bloomington, Indiana

KARIN FORD
Bloomington, Indiana

HERBERT FRANKE
Gauting, Federal Republic
of Germany

LINDA FREY
Missoula, Montana

MARSHA FREY
Manhattan, Kansas

A. v. GABAIN
Anger, Federal Republic of Germany

KAREN GERNANT
Ashland, Oregon

MARTIN GIMM
Köln, Federal Republic of Germany

PETER B. GOLDEN
Newark, New Jersey

GRANT K. GOODMAN
Lawrence, Kansas

CHAUNCEY S. GOODRICH
Santa Barbara, California

L. CARRINGTON GOODRICH
New York, New York

LEONARD H. D. GORDON
West Lafayette, Indiana

KENNETH R. R. GROS LOUIS
Bloomington, Indiana

GREGORY G. GUZMAN
Peoria, Illinois

PÉTER HAJDÚ
Budapest, Hungary

EVA HALASI-KUN
New Milford, Connecticut

TIBOR HALASI-KUN
New Milford, Connecticut

ROBERTE HAMAYON
Paris, France

JAMES R. HAMILTON
Paris, France

ERIC P. HAMP
Chicago, Illinois

GOMBOJAB HANGIN
Bloomington, Indiana

Otto Harrassowitz Verlag
Wiesbaden, Federal Republic
of Germany

SHIRO HATTORI
Yokohama-shi, Japan

HANS-WILHELM HAUSSIG
Berlin, Federal Republic of Germany

BAYMIRZA HAYIT
Köln, Federal Republic of Germany

GYÖRGY HAZAI
Budapest, Hungary

WALTHER HEISSIG
Rheinböllen, Federal Republic
of Germany

JOSEPH HELD
Camden, New Jersey

GEORGE HIBBARD
St. Louis, Missouri

MARGARET HIBBARD
St. Louis, Missouri

Department of History
Indiana University
Bloomington, Indiana

BARRY HOBERMAN
Chapel Hill, North Carolina

CARLETON T. HODGE
Bloomington, Indiana

MINOBU HONDA
Kyoto, Japan

F. W. HOUSEHOLDER
Bloomington, Indiana

EVEN HOVDHAUGEN
Oslo, Norway

RICHARD W. HOWELL
Hizo, Hawaii

PEI HUANG
Youngstown, Ohio

JIRO IKEGAMI
Sapporo, Japan

HALIL INALCIK
Chicago, Illinois

STANLEY INSLER
New Haven, Connecticut

FAHIR IZ
Istanbul, Turkey

ESTHER JACOBSON
Eugene, Oregon

SECHIN JAGCHID
Provo, Utah

JUHA JANHUNEN
Helsinki, Finland

GUNNAR JARRING
Stockholm, Sweden

KARL JETTMAR
Heidelberg, Federal Republic
of Germany

LARS JOHANSON
Mainz, Federal Republic of Germany

AULIS J. JOKI
Helsinki, Finland

HANS-RAINER KAEMPFE
Bloomington, Indiana

GYÖRGY KARA
Budapest, Hungary

JACQUES KARRO
Paris, France

BARBARA KELLNER-HEINKELE
Frankfurt, Federal Republic
of Germany

BÉLA K. KIRÁLY
Highland Lakes, New Jersey

TIMUR KOCAOGLU
Munich, Federal Republic
of Germany

A. N. KONONOV
Moskva, USSR

ZEYNEP KORKMAZ
Ankara, Turkey

LASZLO L. KOVACS
West Lafayette, Indiana

JOHN R. KRUEGER
Bloomington, Indiana

KÁLMÁN KULCSÁR
Budapest, Hungary

OWEN LATTIMORE
Cambridge, England

ILSE LAUDE-CIRTAUTAS
Seattle, Washington

KI-MOON LEE
Seoul, Korea

HSUEH-CHIH LI
Taipei, Taiwan, Republic of China

LOUIS LIGETI
Budapest, Hungary

JOHN V. LOMBARDI
Bloomington, Indiana

COLIN MACKERRAS
Nathan, Australia

SUSAN A. MANGO
Washington, D.C.

PAUL MARER
Bloomington, Indiana

MONICA MASUDA
Täby, Sweden

JUN MATSUMURA
Tokyo, Japan

JOSEF MATUZ
Freiburg, Federal Republic
of Germany

MRS. BERNARDO MENDEL
Bloomington, Indiana

G. M. MEREDITH-OWEN
Toronto, Canada

RUTH I. MESERVE
Bloomington, Indiana

EMANUEL MICKEL
Bloomington, Indiana

ROY ANDREW MILLER
Seattle, Washington

BREON MITCHELL
Ellettsville, Indiana

DAVID NALLE
Washington, D.C.

A. K. NARAIN
Madison, Wisconsin

HOMER A. NEAL
Stony Brook, New York

THUBTEN J. NORBU
Bloomington, Indiana

JERRY NORMAN
Seattle, Washington

PIERRE OBERLING
New York, New York

FELIX J. OINAS
Bloomington, Indiana

HIDEHIRO OKADA
Tokyo, Japan

KURTULUS ÖZTOPCU
Los Angeles, California

WILLIAM S. PEACHY
Columbus, Ohio

G. L. PENROSE
Holland, Michigan

HELMUT PETZOLT
Wiesbaden, Federal Republic
of Germany

NICHOLAS POPPE
Seattle, Washington

FREDERICK A. PRAEGER
Boulder, Colorado

GYÖRGY RÁNKI
Budapest, Hungary

ALO RAUN
Bloomington, Indiana

HENRY H. REMAK
Bloomington, Indiana

JEAN RICHARD
Dijon, France

ANDRÁS RÓNA-TAS
Budapest, Hungary

MORRIS ROSSABI
Cleveland, Ohio

KLAUS SAGASTER
Königswinter, Federal Republic
of Germany

MÁRIA SALGA
Helsinki, Finland

AATOS SALO
Helsinki, Finland

IVAN SANDERS
Stony Brook, New York

ALICE SÁRKÖZI
Budapest, Hungary

A. M. SCERBAK
Leningrad, USSR

ULI SCHAMILOGLU
Bloomington, Indiana

HARTWIG SCHEINHARDT
Germersheim, Federal Republic
of Germany

EDMOND SCHÜTZ
Budapest, Hungary

THOMAS A. SEBEOK
Bloomington, Indiana

GYÖRGY SEBÖK
Bloomington, Indiana

JACK SHINER
Bloomington, Indiana

ELLIOT SPERLING
Bloomington, Indiana

STUART M. SPERRY
Bloomington, Indiana

JÁNOS STARKER
Bloomington, Indiana

GIOVANNI STARY
Venice, Italy

ROBERT C. SUGGS
Alexandria, Virginia

PÄIVIKKI & MATTI SUOJANEN
Bloomington, Indiana

MAGDALENA TATÁR
Oslo, Norway

ERIKA TAUBE
Leipzig, German Democratic
Republic

MANFRED TAUBE
Leipzig, German Democratic
Republic

S. Y. TENG
Bloomington, Indiana

HANS B. THORELLI
Gosport, Indiana

ANDREAS TIETZE
Vienna, Austria

MICHAEL UNDERDOWN
Kew, Australia

CATHERINE URAY-KÖHALMI
Budapest, Hungary

GÉZA URAY
Budapest, Hungary

ALOIS VAN TONGERLOO
Herent, Belgium

CHARLES D. VAN TUYL
Porter, Oklahoma

ISTVÁN VÁSÁRY
Budapest, Hungary

VERONICA VEIT
Bonn, Federal Republic of Germany

HANS-PETER VIETZE
Berlin, German Democratic Republic

BENJAMIN E. WALLACKER
Davis, California

HARTMUT WALRAVENS
Hamburg, Federal Republic
of Germany

MARY FRANCES WEIDLICH
Silver Spring, Maryland

HERMAN B WELLS
Bloomington, Indiana

ALBERT WERTHEIM
Bloomington, Indiana

BO WICKMAN
Uppsala, Sweden

GEORGE M. WILSON
Bloomington, Indiana

GEORGE W. WILSON
Bloomington, Indiana

STEPHEN A. WURM
Canberra, Australia

PETER ZIEME
Berlin, German Democratic Republic

AFTERWORD

In 1976, on his sixtieth birthday, Professor Sinor was presented with a Festschrift (*Tractata Altaica. Denis Sinor,* edited by Walther Heissig, John R. Krueger, Felix J. Oinas, and Edmond Schütz, Wiesbaden: Otto Harrassowitz, 1976, 775 pp.) to celebrate the occasion; now, ten years later, it has been decided that a complete bibliography of his long and distinguished career should be published and presented to him.

I should like to take this opportunity to thank the Board of Editors for this Bibliography, namely: Gustav Bayerle, Chairman of the Department of Uralic and Altaic Studies at Indiana University; Gyula Décsy, professor of Uralic studies in the same department; and Emanuel Mickel, Chairman of French and Italian and Director of the Medieval Studies Program at Indiana University. I would also like to thank Mrs. Karin Ford, Administrative Assistant of the Department of Uralic and Altaic Studies, for her assistance and Mrs. K. Gartland and Miss P. Lepley for their help in typing.

Much of the work toward compiling this Bibliography was greatly simplified by the extensive records kept by DS. Still, there are areas in the Bibliography which may not be complete: some reviews of books authored or edited by DS may have been unintentionally overlooked; some lectures were undoubtedly missed. It has, however, been my intention from the very beginning to make this bibliography as complete as possible and I, naturally, assume responsibility. DS's career is still very active; many items are at the publishers at this moment. Those of you who know DS have no doubt heard him forecast his plans for "1997, during which I will write on this topic and in 2004 such and such is scheduled". His love of scholarship and the desire to spend most waking hours engaged in his "favorite" activity make this bibliography, in reality, a reflection of his work only from the year 1937 when his first publication appeared up to February 1986 when this manuscript was sent to the printer. We all wish Professor Sinor not only a very happy seventieth birthday but also a continued active and productive scholarly life in which he may realize his dreams.

Indiana University   RUTH I. MESERVE

40 ans apres ! JUNE 1984

ARCADIA BIBLIOGRAPHICA VIRORUM ERUDITORUM

ISSN 0195-7163

Fasciculus 1   *Karl Heinrich Menges Bibliographie.* Compiled by STEVEN E. HEGAARD. 1979. 57 pp. ISBN 3-447-01835/6. US $15.

Fasciculus 2   *Alo Raun Bibliography.* Compiled by GUSTAV BAYERLE. 1980. 29 pp. ISBN 0-931922-02-X. US $15.

Fasciculus 3   *Erich Kunze Bibliographie.* Mit Unterstützung der Friedrich-Ebert-Stiftung. 1980. 33 pp. ISBN 0-931922-07-0. US $15.

Fasciculus 4   *Felix Johannes Oinas Bibliography.* Compiled by R. F. FELDSTEIN. 1981. 51 pp. ISBN 0-931922-03-8. US $15.

Fasciculus 5   *Helmut Hoffman Bibliography.* Compiled by MICHAEL WALTER. 1982. 28 pp. ISBN 0-931922-13-5. US $15.

Fasciculus 6   *Fred W. Householder Bibliography.* Compiled by SALMAN H. AL-ANI. 1984. 37 pp. ISBN 0-931922-16-X. US $15.

Fasciculus 7   *Ferenc Fabricius-Kovács Bibliography.* With support of the Hungarian Cultural Association of Chicago. Compiled by MIKLÓS KONTRA. 1984. 41 pp. ISBN 0-931922-18-6. US $15.

Fasciculus 8   *György Lakó Bibliographie.* Zusammengestellt von EDITH VÉRTES. 1985. 37 pp. ISBN 0-931922-21-6. US $15.

Fasciculus 9   *Denis Sinor Bibliography.* Compiled by RUTH I. MESERVE. 1986. 65 pp. ISBN 0-931922-12-7. US $15.

Distributed by:

EUROLINGUA
P.O. Box 101
Bloomington, IN 47402-0101
USA